❖
_____

The Southern Tradition

The William E. Massey Sr. Lectures in the
History of American Civilization
1993

The Southern
✛ Tradition

The Achievement and Limitations of
an American Conservatism

Eugene D. Genovese

Harvard University Press

Cambridge, Massachusetts
London, England

First Harvard University Press paperback edition, 1996

Library of Congress Cataloging-in-Publication Data

Genovese, Eugene D., 1930–
    The southern tradition: the achievement and limitations of an American conservatism / Eugene D. Genovese.
        p. cm.—(The William E. Massey Sr. lectures in the history of American civilization; 1993)
    Includes index.
    ISBN 0–674–82527–6 (cloth)
    ISBN 0-674-82528-4 (pbk.)
    1. Conservatism—Southern States—History. 2. Southern States—Politics and government. I. Title. II. Series.
F209.5.G46 1994
320.975—dc20
                                                                                        94–4586
                                                                                        CIP

In gratitude:

Louis A. Ferleger
Robert L. Paquette
—friends in need

Contents

Preface

> "The South is the region that history has happened to."
>
> —Richard Weaver

I speak and write uneasily on the southern (conservative) tradition, an unpopular subject that has been gnawing at me for more than three decades. I am a native New Yorker who was born and raised in New York City and who has spent almost all except the last eight of his sixty-three years as a resident of New York State. My pretensions to being a southerner—for, alas, pretensions are all they are—rest on my having become fascinated with southern history while an undergraduate at Brooklyn College and on having settled my heart in Dixie soon thereafter. Certainly, I am devoted to the sentiment expressed in the bumper sticker: "Get your heart in Dixie or get your ass out!" There are a great many reasons for my southern partisanship, the most important of which arose from my early recognition that the people of the South, across lines of race, class, and sex, are as generous, gracious, courteous, decent—in a word, civilized—as any people it has ever been my privilege to get to know. And yes, I know that I am open to the charge made against all converts of being *plus royaliste que le roi, plus catholique que le Pape.*

As for my being a conservative—a label applied to me frequently these days by people who understand nothing—I have always expressed admiration for much in conservative thought and have many friends among southern conservatives, not to mention neoconservatives, free-market conservatives, and demonstrably crazy conservatives. But I know of no one in any of those camps who does not smile when hearing me described as any kind of a conservative. This book has been written by an outsider—a sympathetic, respectful, and I hope fair-minded outsider, but an outsider nonetheless.

I hear often, as do some others who come out of the Marxist Left, that we just love to cuddle with southern conservatives because they, too, criticize capitalism and beat up on the bourgeoisie. Apparently, we find them soul-brothers despite a few presumably inconsequential ideological and political differences. Maybe. But more important matters are at stake than the games intellectuals play. From the beginning of my academic career in the 1950s, I have argued that the Left would have to learn some hard lessons from southern conservatives if it were ever to rescue itself from the overt totalitarianism of Stalinism and the disguised totalitarian tendencies that infect left-liberalism and social democracy. The hard lessons I have had in mind, which especially concern the Left's rosy view of human nature and the irrationalities of its radical egalitarianism, may be gleaned from this book. Still, a proper exposition would require a different kind of book. For "a decent respect to the opinions of mankind" requires that those of us who spent our lives in a political movement that piled up tens of millions of corpses to sustain a futile cause and hideous political regimes have a few questions to answer.

My reasons for choosing "the southern tradition" as the topic for the Massey Lectures derive from but transcend such considerations. I am alarmed at the "modernization" that is transforming the South. Doubtless, the transformation has much to recommend it, especially with respect to long overdue if incomplete justice for black people. But I increasingly suspect that its desirable features are coming at a price northerners as well as southerners, blacks as well as whites, will rue having to pay and need not pay. That price includes a neglect of, or contempt for, the history of southern whites, without which some of the more distinct and noble features of American national life must remain incomprehensible.

The northern victory in 1865 silenced a discretely southern interpretation of American history and national identity, and it promoted a contemptuous dismissal of all things southern as nasty, racist, immoral, and intellectually inferior. The northern victory did carry out a much too belated abolition of slavery. But it also sanctified northern institutions and intentions, which included the unfettered expansion of a bourgeois world view and the suppression of alternate visions of social order. In consequence, from that day to this, the southern-conservative critique of modern gnosticism has been wrongly equated with racism and white supremacy.

Rarely these days, even on southern campuses, is it possible to acknowledge the achievements of the white people of the South. The history of the Old South is now often taught at leading universities, when it is taught at all, as a prolonged guilt-trip, not to say a prologue to the history of Nazi Germany. Courses on the history of the modern South ignore an array of movements and individuals, including the Fugitive poets, the Agrarians, Richard Weaver, and such intellectually impressive successors as the late M. E. Bradford and those engaged in today's political and ideological wars. These nonpersons have nevertheless constituted a movement that, by any reasonable standard, ought to be acknowledged for its outstanding contributions to American social, political, and cultural thought.

To speak positively about any part of this southern tradition is to invite charges of being a racist and an apologist for slavery and segregation. We are witnessing a cultural and political atrocity—an increasingly successful campaign by the media and an academic elite to strip young white southerners, and arguably black southerners as well, of their heritage, and, therefore, their identity. They are being taught to forget their forebears or to remember them with shame. Still, we may doubt that many young southerners believe that Jefferson Davis and Alexander Stephens, John C. Calhoun and James Henley Thornwell, Robert E. Lee and Stonewall Jackson were other than admirable men. It is one thing to silence people, another to convince them. And to silence them on matters central to their self-respect and dignity is to play a dangerous game—to build up in them harsh resentments that, sooner or later, are likely to explode and bring out their worst.

Recall that great speech by Martin Luther King in which he evoked a vision of the descendants of slaves and of slaveholders, sitting together on the hills of Georgia as southern brothers. That vision will be realized when, and only when, those descendants, black and white, can meet with mutual respect and appreciation for the greatness, as well as the evil, that has gone into the making of the South. Black Americans have good reason to protest vehemently against the disgraceful way in which their history has been taught or, worse, ignored, and to demand a record of the nobility and heroism of the black struggle for freedom and justice. But that record dare not include the falsification or obliteration of the noble and heroic features of the white South. To teach the one without the other is to invite deepening racial animosity and murderous conflict, not merely or even primarily in the South but in the North. For it is worth noting that our most vicious urban explosions are occurring in the "progressive" North and on the West Coast, not in the "bigoted" and "reactionary" South.

It is one thing to demand—and it must be demanded—that white southerners repudiate white supremacy. It is quite another to demand that they deny the achievements of their own people in a no less heroic struggle to build a civilization in a wilderness and to create the modern world's first great republic—to demand that they repent in sackcloth and ashes not only for undeniable enormities, but for the finest and most generous features of southern life. Recall the words of W. E. B. Du Bois' "Of the Wings of Atalanta" in *The Souls of Black Folk:*

> Once, they say, even Atlanta slept dull and drowsy at the foothills of the Alleghanies, until the iron baptism of war awakened her with its sullen waters, aroused and maddened her, and left her listening to the sea. . . .
>
> It is a hard thing to live haunted by the ghost of an untrue dream; to see the wide vision of empire fade into real ashes and dirt; to feel the pang of the conquered, and yet know that with all the Bad that fell on one black day, something was vanquished that deserved to live, something killed that in justice had not dared to die; to know that with the Right that triumphed, triumphed something of Wrong, something sordid and mean, something less than the broadest and best. All this is bitter hard . . .

It is dangerous as well as wrong to obscure the genuinely tragic dimension of southern history—the extent to which courageous, God-fearing, honorable people rendered themselves complicit in slavery, segregation, and racism and ended up in defeat and degradation. That historical lesson speaks to all people in all times, warning of the corrupt and cruel tendencies inherent in our common humanity and the ease with which the social relations and institutions we sustain may encourage the most destructive aspects of our nature.

What you have as heritage,
Take now as task;
For thus you will make it your own.

—Goethe, *Faust*

Introduction

Tradition is the living faith of the dead, traditionalism is the
dead faith of the living.

— Jaroslav Pelikan, *The Vindication of Tradition*

The principal tradition of the South—the mainstream of its cultural
development—has been quintessentially conservative. Richard
Weaver and his successors have had every right to speak simply of
the southern tradition, notwithstanding the many important liberal
and left-wing challenges that have enriched southern history. I focus
here on the white South not only because it has been politically and
ideologically dominant but because its principal features are, at this
moment, being obscured if not ignored. A full assessment of southern history, which cannot be essayed here, would have to pay careful
attention to the black South and to the extent to which the two have
been organically related and yet distinct.

Those who despise the southern tradition have inadvertently conceded its historical preponderance. Repeatedly, they have celebrated
one or another "New South" that, ostensibly, has finally joined
mainstream America. Understandably, liberals seek to silence a
southern conservatism that has, from its origins, constituted America's most impressive native-born critique of our national develop-

1

ment, of liberalism, and of the more disquieting features of the modern world. That critique nonetheless continues to have much to offer those who recognize that the United States and all Western civilization face fateful choices in a period of worldwide upheaval and uncertainty.

Here we confront a special kind of conservatism that has little in common with market-oriented bourgeois ideologies. For as M. E. Bradford has said, one may be a southerner and lay claims to being a conservative and yet not be a southern conservative.[1] To grasp the distinction, we must begin with an understanding of the southern conservatives' claim to being heirs to a "tradition" that embodies the essentials of the history of a South they regard as a worthy embodiment of Western Christian civilization. It also requires that we begin with an understanding of the place of poetry and myth in the elaboration of that history.

The southern conservatives' insistence upon the importance of poetry to the struggle for a just society has, despite repeated misunderstandings, nothing to do with a demand for political poetry. They have turned to poetry for an aesthetic vision of an older Christian view of the flowering of the personality within a corporate structure, and they have counterposed that vision to the personalism of modern bourgeois individualist ideology. Allen Tate, John Crowe Ransom, Robert Penn Warren, and their colleagues shared with William Butler Yeats, T. S. Eliot, W. H. Auden, and other leading poets of our century a passionate desire to restore myth to its proper place in literature. They agreed with Auden on the need for myth in a modern society in which "men are no longer supported by tradition without being aware of it." And they agreed with him that men must now do self-consciously what had been done for them by "family, custom, church, and state." Like Eliot but unlike Auden and Yeats, they focused on the moral rather than the psychological uses of myth.[2]

These twentieth-century poets did not turn to myth out of a belief in the truth of the myths themselves, for they recognized the content as simultaneously true and false. They did so out of a desire for order and objective standards. As Lillian Feder has wisely observed, myths express our deepest self-deceptions as well as our most admirable aspirations: "Only in these fantastic forms can man reveal certain of his fears, his desires, and his tentative apprehension of the real world and his own nature. What he declares about himself in myth can be experienced in no other way, for the expository language of rational thought cannot contain it."[3]

Tate's thesis that the southern mode of imagination has been characteristically rhetorical, rather than dialectical, reflects this perception of the power of myth, much as does Ransom's thesis that significant myths are at bottom religious and, indeed, dogmatic. Tate's finest poems, "The Mediterranean," "Aeneas at Washington," and "Ode to the Confederate Dead," draw on Roman sources in the manner of his antebellum southern predecessors to express, in Feder's words, man's "yearning for a nation that embodies ethical and spiritual ideals which can involve his deepest feelings."[4] This perspective supports and enriches John Shelton Reed's interpretation of *I'll Take My Stand* as a platform for southern nationalism, much as it recalls Henry Timrod's celebration of the birth of the Confederacy in his poem "Ethnogenesis."[5]

Thus Bradford wrote, "All our social myths presupposed some version of the corporate life—that man is a social being, fulfilled only in the natural associations built upon common experience, upon the ties of blood and friendship, common enterprise, resistance to common enemies, and a common faith."[6] Bradford elaborated on the Roman roots of the "social bond individualism" that Weaver invoked to capture the southern conservatives' version of Christian individualism and to distinguish it from the bourgeois individualism associated with the Renaissance and the French Enlightenment.[7]

For Bradford, social bond individualism reflects not a secular state of mind but that which Weaver called "the older religiousness of the South" rooted in piety rather than dogma. "A good Roman of the old school," Bradford wrote, "had personal pride and a considerable sense of honor. His was a shame culture, dominated by intense and personally felt loyalties to family, clan, and individual. Commitment to Rome had its roots in, and was not separable from, these attachments . . . The Roman was not an individual as we understand the term."[8]

Tate set the standard by asserting that he and his colleagues had "a notion that tradition is not simply a fact that must constantly be defended." Such a defense Tate dismissed as dogma, asserting that "dogma as rationality is certainly a half-religion and is on the way to becoming science or practicality." He did not doubt that tradition could always be defended, but he insisted that its restoration poses a much more difficult task, which the steady industrialization, urbanization, and liberalization of the South has been making especially difficult.[9]

In claiming a "tradition," southern conservatives appeal to history in order to interpret the Old South as a religiously grounded society.[10] That society, they argue, grew out of people who settled Virginia and the Carolinas not to build a City on a Hill but to acquire freeholds and, with them, the status and self-respect appropriate to Englishmen. "We were," Bradford wrote, "republican long before we were a republic."[11] Bradford's focus on freeholds resists secular interpretation, for it assumes that those who could acquire property thereby positioned themselves to exercise free will to choose the good. And it further assumes that their notion of the good corresponded to the Christian virtues of a Western civilization whose conscious heirs they were.

"Tradition" is here understood as an embodiment of "givens" that must constantly be fought for, recovered in each generation, and adjusted to new conditions. Tate, in a remark that has become infamous among those inclined to wooden readings, declared that southerners must take possession of their tradition "by violence."[12] He was saying little more than what Goethe had said in the celebrated passage in *Faust* on heritage as task.[13] T. S. Eliot made the meaning clearer than Tate himself did:

> Yet if the only form of tradition, of handing down, consisted in following the ways of the immediate generation before us in a blind or timid adherence to its successes, "tradition" should positively be discouraged. We have seen many such simple currents soon lost in the sand; and novelty is better than repetition. Tradition is a matter of much wider significance. It cannot be inherited, and if you want it you must obtain it by great labour. It involves in the first place the historical sense, . . . and the historical sense involves a perception not only of the pastness of the past, but of its presence; the historical sense compels a man to write not merely with his own generation in his bones, but with a feeling that the whole of the literature of Europe from Homer and within it the whole of the literature of his own country has a simultaneous existence and composes a simultaneous order. This historical sense, which is a sense of the timeless as well as of the temporal and of the timeless and the temporal together, is what makes a writer traditional. And it is at the same time what makes a writer most acutely conscious of his place in time, of his own contemporaneity.[14]

Southern conservatives, as "traditionalists," have espoused a "tradition" to be fought for, not a "traditionalism" cast in stone and worshiped as an idol.

Although rooted in early American history, southern conservatism as a movement of self-conscious intellectuals came to national attention in the 1930s with the "Southern Agrarians," led primarily by such outstanding literary figures as Tate, Ransom, Warren, Donald Davidson, John Gould Fletcher, and Andrew Lytle.[15] It announced itself to the world in the fiery manifesto *I'll Take My Stand* and achieved its most comprehensive theoretical formulation after the Second World War in the work of Richard Weaver.[16] Carried forward under Bradford's intellectual and political aegis, it enjoys the support of a talented group of scholars, writers, and social critics.

Talent and vision notwithstanding, southern conservatives are still having trouble building a mass political movement of their own, even though they are influencing—some would say tormenting—the larger national movement that miscalls itself "conservative." Still, the southern-conservative message is beginning to resonate well beyond the South even as it recedes within it. And despite continued temptations and bad moments, their movement shows signs of exorcizing the racism that has marred much of its history.[17]

On these matters, criticism of the draft of this book compels me to anticipate three demands for a clarification of premises. The first concerns the present political condition of the traditionalist Right and its southern component. The second concerns the relation between the positive and negative features of southern conservatism and the extent to which the two may be separated not merely analytically but politically. The third concerns the centrality of racial justice to the political struggles that constitute the underlying theme of this book.

During the 1992 presidential elections, the traditionalists rallied behind Patrick Buchanan's challenge to George Bush in the Republican primary. They did not do badly as such challenges to a sitting president go, but neither did they do as well as they expected or others feared. Among the reasons for their failure to receive as many votes as expected was their inability to carry much of the "Religious Right" with them. The most prominent of the politically engaged religious leaders stayed with Bush. In the contest between Bush and Bill Clinton, the traditionalists split three ways: for Bush or Clinton as the lesser evil or for a day's fishing.

Nor have their fortunes improved much since then. No few among their number would like to see a split with the Republican establishment and the creation of a new party. But Buchanan, the only man of political stature on the horizon who might carry their banner effectively, may wish to continue the fight within the Republican Party, where he has poor prospects. And within the party, the one well organized group capable of influencing policy in his preferred direction consists of religious leaders who give no sign of supporting his renewed candidacy.

Like the Agrarians before them, the southern conservatives and other traditionalists appear to be isolated intellectuals who wield only a modest influence over public opinion through magazines and the efforts of able newspaper columnists like the redoubtable Samuel Francis.[18] Indeed, they continue to have difficulty making up their minds whether to play Cassandra and keep the faith pure, unsullied, and politically ineffective or to fight for a place in a basically centrist Republican coalition. For whatever my opinion is worth, they are potentially stronger than they know, and, if they ever get themselves organized, they could emerge with surprising strength.

So much for my opinion. Predictions of political success are not the strong point of a man who until only a few years ago thought that socialism was the wave of the future and never dreamed that the Soviet Union could collapse. The argument of this book does not depend upon the political fortunes of the southern conservatives. Rather, it insists that their critique of modernism—and, by extension, of postmodernism—contains much of intrinsic value that will have to be incorporated in the world view of any political movement, inside or outside the principal political parties, that expects to arrest our plunge into moral decadence and national decline.

Hence the second criticism. I argue throughout that the southern conservatives today build on an impressive critique of modern life and American institutions formulated by their forebears during the late eighteenth and nineteenth centuries. I argue, further, that the staying power of that critique resulted primarily from the social relations spawned by slavery, the end of which removed the social foundation for sustained opposition to bourgeois hegemony. The principle features of the southern world view—for example, its republicanism—had roots in the history of Western civilization, most notably in the history of Britain, and cannot be regarded as an ideological projection of slavery. Indeed, the proslavery theorists always insisted that the Old South was a continuation of the mainstream of the development of Christendom and that the North was a heretical deviation. In my previous work I have, in effect, agreed with the essentials of their argument. But that very argument stressed the centrality of organic social relations to cultural development. In other words, slavery made possible the defense and preservation of a system of values that was unraveling in a North based on bourgeois social relations that undermined all tradition. If so, it follows that the recreation of tradition requires new forms of social relations appropriate to the complexities of the modern world.

It is nonetheless fair to ask: Do not southern conservatives plunge into romanticism and nostalgia in believing that the "traditional values" they continue to defend could possibly be sustained without the original social base? To turn the question on its head: Since—let us pray—all would agree that slavery was an enormity that deserved to perish, is not the destruction of those traditional values the price we have had to pay for a desired result?

Southern conservatives and other philosophical idealists seem to think that the values could be defended or restored despite the triumph of bourgeois social relations and an attendant, self-revolutionizing economic system that has historically proven itself a solvent of those very values. I wish them luck but do not believe a word of it. With the proslavery theorists, as well as with Marx, I believe social relations, whether master/slave or capitalist/worker, set definite limits to what may be accomplished in the polity and the culture. Consequently, I argue in Chapter 3 that, to the extent to which the southern-conservative critique of modernism remains valid, the struggle for its political realization must depend upon the outcome of a struggle to restructure social relations.

Finally, I have not dwelt upon the racist legacy of the southern tradition because I assume that readers will join me in taking it as a given. Rather, I have suggested that the realization of the finest values of the southern tradition requires a total break with its legacy of racism, and that, in particular, the social restructuring at issue could not proceed in a racially stratified way without destroying, in a single stroke, the republicanism that southern conservatives themselves insist is necessary to social order. On this matter I have expressed my hopes more readily than my fears. But the potential danger ought to be obvious. If a political movement in defense of the best of the southern tradition does not include blacks as well as whites—if it is not deeply committed to racial equity and justice—it will degenerate into barbarism as fast as we can swallow our spit. No crystal ball is required to tell us that every racist cockroach in the woodwork will rush to join the ranks, and that only the most sainted political leader would be willing or able to turn his back on his constituency.

That miserable end is not fated. We—those outside as well as inside the southern conservative camp—will have no one to blame if we proceed in a manner guaranteed to effect a self-fulfilling prophecy.

1 ❖

Lineaments of the Southern Tradition

Here I am tempted to construct a little fairy tale. Once upon a time, there was a bumbling and kind-hearted old father named Science, and he had a smart, brawny son who found the father's way of life dull, and so set forth to make his fortune. Not far on his journey he met a beautiful golden-haired lady with a bewitching smile. Her name was Money. Now Money had a bad reputation in certain quarters, especially among old, stuffy folk, and it was even rumored that she had borne several bastards. But bastards or no, she had never lost her girlishly lissome figure, delicious complexion, promising smile, and eye for brawny young fellows. Of course this young fellow, having been raised in so retired a way, knew nothing of the gossip about the lady. So they got married and lived happily ever after—at least, until right now—for he was blind to her little private diversions and was wrapped up in a beautiful, thriving little son who grew as fast as a beanstalk and whose name was Business Culture. I forgot to tell you that the brawny young fellow who married the durable lady was named Technology.

—Robert Penn Warren, *Democracy and Poetry*

"There is ground for declaring," Richard Weaver wrote in *Ideas Have Consequences*, "that modern man has become a moral idiot . . . For four centuries every man has been not only his own priest but his own professor of ethics, and the consequence is an anarchy which threatens even that minimum consensus of value necessary to the political state."[1] Weaver was openly attacking capitalism and modern bourgeois society, as well as socialism and communism. Thus, he followed the Southern Agrarians back to the ideas of John Randolph of Roanoke and John Taylor of Caroline, whose thought he especially appreciated for its commitment to a widespread dispersal of property and political power and opposition to the allocation of wealth by political means.

Building upon such tenets of southern conservatism, Weaver focused on the indispensability of private property to a free society, while he rejected the prevailing forms of corporate property as destructive of the very private property they claim to represent. He linked the rise of the intrusive modern state to an industrial order that increasingly undermined the modernist concept of individual moral accountability. Southern conservatives have always been deeply critical of modernism, although they have accepted much of the material and technological advances of the modern world and especially its emphasis on the dignity of the individual personality. It should be enough to recall the extraordinary contributions of Tate and Ransom to the movement in poetry and literary criticism led by T. S. Eliot and designed to capture the best in modernity and to purge the worst. Southern conservatives have condemned not science, reason, material progress, and individualism, but, rather, the cult of scientism, atheistic and pantheistic rationalism, and a material progress that has resulted in the alienation of the individual from self and society.

Southern conservatives do not reject science; they reject its messianic pretensions. They have responded in the manner of T. S. Eliot, whose *Waste Land* (1922) excoriated, in the words of Lewis P. Simpson, "the world historical goal of the scientists in an unprecedented bloodletting." As poets, the Agrarians sought "to define existence through enactments of the imagination instead of through observation and experiment" and therefore sought "to establish the power of poetry as knowledge." Or as Robert Wooster Stallman put it, Tate, Ransom, and their colleagues accepted Eliot's major premise and focused their poetry and literary criticism on "the dislocation of modern sensibility—the issue of our glorification of the scientific vision at the expense of the aesthetic vision."[2]

The Agrarians deserve belated tribute for having been, as it were, premature environmentalists. The rape of the environment was a leading theme in *I'll Take My Stand* and its sequel, *Who Owns America?* Fifty years later Cleanth Brooks, Lyle Lanier, Andrew Lytle, and Robert Penn Warren recalled the early efforts of the Agrarians to sound the tocsin on environmental issues and reaffirmed their own commitment in white heat. Their successors, in the pages of such journals as *Chronicles: A Magazine of American Culture* and *Southern Partisan* and elsewhere have forcefully carried forward the Agrarians' denunciation of the rape of nature by soulless economic systems.[3]

Significantly, for the Agrarians, as for T. S. Eliot, the roots of the protest against the destruction of the environment, which informed their critique of slavery as well as of the capitalist exploitation of man and nature, lay in a Christian world view. Thus Allen Tate:

> The South, afflicted with the curse of slavery—a curse like that of Original Sin, for which no single person is responsible—had to be destroyed, the good along with the evil. The old order had a great deal of good, one of the "goods" being the result of the evil; for slavery itself entailed a certain responsibility which the capitalist

employer in free societies did not need to exercise if it was not his will to do so . . .

The evil of slavery was twofold, for the "peculiar Institution" not only used human beings for a purpose for which God had not intended them; it made it possible for the white man to misuse and exploit nature itself for his own power and glory.[4]

The same religious world view has shaped the southern conservatives' attitude toward individualism, which they do not condemn but celebrate. But they do condemn an individualism torn loose from family, community, and civic responsibility—an individualism that has metamorphosed into egocentrism, personal irresponsibility, and a loss of civic discipline. They have, that is, counterposed an older Christian notion of a God-given dignity of the personality to the bourgeois notion of the individual as the center of the universe.[5] For them, the very dignity of the personality requires roots in the community and, above all, the family.

The southern-conservative critique of individualism shares much with that of other Christians who have refused to capitulate to theological liberalism. Spokesmen for the Catholic Church and the Orthodox Presbyterian Church, among others, have drawn on Saint Augustine's denunciation of self-love and the contempt for God inherent in the claim that He is a limited Being. In particular, they have stressed the inviolability of the family—"the society of a man's household," as Pope Leo XIII described it—as anterior to state and nation, with the individual head of household as the authoritative officer of its members. In this spirit, Pope John Paul II has recently denounced "self-love carried to the point of contempt for God and neighbor, a self-love which leads to an unbridled affirmation of self-interest and which refuses to be limited by any demand of justice." The market and its attendant "radical capitalist ideology," he added in words not much different from those of *I'll*

Take My Stand, "encourage instincts that lead to *consumer attitudes* and *life-styles*" devoid of criteria for the good life and the requirements for a "mature personality." In words that were heard frequently in the Old South and resonate today in black churches and well beyond, Pope John Paul II thundered against "having" rather than "being."[6]

Catholic spokesmen, like southern-conservative spokesmen, do not attack markets per se. They recognize that markets, especially in earlier times, have served as meeting places for face-to-face exchange of goods and had a civilizing function. Rather, they protest against the transformation of the market, especially with the rise of a world market, into an impersonal arena in which human relations themselves are treated as commodities. From a different point of view, Marx's famous set piece "The Fetishism of Commodities" illuminates the ramifications of this transformation with unparalleled insight and depth.[7]

Protestants may prefer the version offered by James Henley Thornwell, the orthodox Calvinist recognized as among the greatest of nineteenth-century southern theologians, who continues to be honored among orthodox Presbyterians: "The human race is not an aggregation of separate and independent atoms, but constitutes an organic whole, with a common life springing from a common ground. There is a unity in the whole species; there is a point in which . . . they are all modified and conditioned . . . There is in man what we may call a common nature . . . Birth consequently does not absolutely begin, but only individualizes humanity."[8]

Smith, like Thornwell before him, ranks as a political as well as theological conservative, but those who cavil on that account may turn to Karl Barth, a product of the Calvinist tradition, a man of the socialist Left, and one of the greatest Protestant theologians of the twentieth century:

Thus the Christian approach surpasses both individualism and collectivism. The church knows and recognizes the "interest" of the individual and of the whole, but it resists them both when they want to have the last word. It subordinates them to the being of the citizen, the being of the civil community before the law, over which neither the individuals nor the "whole" are to hold sway, but which they are to seek after, to find and to serve—always with a view to limiting and preserving human life.[9]

The Agrarians, most notably Tate, sought, in the words of Lewis P. Simpson, to transcend the "transference of mind into the self by reversing mind and society as models of history." Tate, in other words, sought to spiritualize the secular rather than capitulate to the secularization of the spiritual. For as Simpson adds, Tate recognized the ultimate impossibility of the project and the need to appeal well beyond the South to accomplish anything at all. That the project is ultimately impossible remains moot. Those who despair might well consider John Lukacs' argument that "the spiritualization of matter" constitutes a principal tendency in contemporary thought and sensibility.[10]

The Agrarians consciously sought a national and international audience for their message. Donald Davidson wrote of the Agrarians' crusade, "For brevity, I might call it the cause of civilized society, as we have known it in the Western world, against the new barbarism of science and technology controlled and directed by the modern power state. In this sense, the cause of the South was and is the cause of Western civilization itself."[11] Weaver, writing more than a decade later, noted that many of the Agrarians had moved to the North, as he himself had done. For in truth, the Agrarians, as intellectuals who appealed primarily to a folk culture, had few people to talk to in the South, having isolated themselves by their very intellectuality. Especially during the Great Depression, they fled in quest of a broader base among conservative critics of finance capitalism, whose numbers were increasing in the North. In defense of the Agrarians, Weaver argued, echoing Tate and Ransom, "In the battle against anti-humanist forces one does not desert by changing his locale for the plain reason that the battle is world wide."[12]

Notwithstanding a determination to find a general audience in Christendom, southern conservatives have necessarily argued that *I'll Take My Stand* be understood, first and foremost, as a southern book. John Shelton Reed has made a strong case for its being a rallying call to southern nationalists who were intent upon achieving as much regional autonomy as possible and who were hankering after a second secession even as they knew it to be out of the question.[13]

Bradford pointedly objected to all attempts, whether friendly or hostile, to desectionalize *I'll Take My Stand* and to lift it out of time. He had no wish to deny the Agrarians' connection to European culture or to the best features of northern culture for that matter, and he assuredly did not want to isolate southern conservatives politically. Instead, he focused on the specific contribution of the South to the broader transatlantic culture of the Christian West. Thus, he stressed the historical contribution of men like John Randolph of Roanoke and even of Thomas Jefferson in his sometime incarnation as an "anti-Hamiltonian, antistatist, conservative Democrat." The republican tradition held pride of place for Bradford, who applauded the leaders of the Old South:

Neither were they high Tory champions of an aristocratic regime on the continental European model. Community was their prior ideal—an informally hierarchical social organism in which all Southerners (including the Negro insofar as the survival of the community permitted) had a sense of investment and participation. In brief, a patriarchal world of families, pre- or noncapitalist *because* familial, located, pious, and "brotherly"; agrarian in order not to produce the alienated, atomistic individual to whom abstractly familial totalitarianism can appeal; classically republican because that system of government best allowed for the multiplicity that was the nation while at the same time permitting the agrarian culture of families to flourish unperturbed.[14]

Allen Tate and Donald Davidson shed light on this tension between the regional and the universal in a discussion of poetic form. Building on Tate's dictum that the form requires the myth, Davidson explained:

The images and symbols, in fact the total economy of the poem, require the support of a tradition based upon a generally diffused belief. A skeptical poetry was a contradiction in terms—an impossibility, at best artificiality rather than art. And since a tradition could not flourish without a society to support it, the natural step was to remember that after all we were Southerners and that the South still possessed at least the remnants, maybe more than the remnants, of a traditional, believing society.[15]

Tate, writing in 1945, struck back at the endless charges of provincialism aimed at the Agrarians by their liberal critics: "Regionalism without civilization—which means with us, regionalism without the classical-Christian culture—becomes provincialism; and world regionalism becomes world provincialism." Tate defined provincialism as a "state of mind in which regional men lose their origins in the past and its continuity into the present, and begin every day as if there had been no yesterday." Davidson, quoting Tate at length, agreed that the Agrarians upheld a classical and Christian world based upon a regional consciousness that championed "honor, truth, imagination, human dignity, and limited acquisitiveness." Only such a vision, Tate and Davidson proclaimed, could rescue Western civilization, America, and the South itself from their present corruption.[16]

Whatever slim hopes the Agrarians may have had of arresting the industrialization of the South sixty years ago, their successors have none. John Shelton Reed has said it all in two sentences: "It is no longer a matter of defending a 'Southern way of life' against industrialism. Increasingly, that way of life *is* industrialism."[17] Hopes for the maintenance or restoration of cherished values now rest with the possibilities for the growth of new types of communities in cities and suburbs. Bradford even suggested, regrettably without elaboration, that the technological revolution in communications might be turned to advantage by those who value privacy and a responsible individualism that resists state intervention in community, family, and personal life.

The political question, therefore, is no longer regional or even national but universal. In *Why the South Will Survive*, a reaffirmation by fifteen southerners published on the occasion of the fiftieth anniversary of *I'll Take My Stand*, Clyde Wilson wrote, "One of the implications running through this book is that the South is, or ought to be, of compelling interest to that thoughtful minority concerned with conserving what is left of Christianity and Western Civilization."[18]

Russell Kirk, a northern traditionalist, has drawn attention to the "provincial" side of southern conservatism or, rather, of the conservative South, describing its ethos as "a set of assumptions and characteristics, only dimly expressed but none the less real, which give the Southern conservative tradition its curious tenacity." Kirk refers to "a preference for the slow processes of natural change, distinguished from artificial innovation—the spirit of 'easy does it.'" But he concludes, "The modern South cannot be said to obey consciously conservative ideas—only conservative instincts, exposed to all the corruption that instinct unlit by principle encounters in a literate age." Kirk then expresses horror at the decline from John Randolph of Roanoke to Theodore Bilbo, the vulgar racist who represented Mississippi in the United States Senate a half-century ago.[19]

Kirk surely knows that southern conservatives despised Bilbo as a demagogue whose socioeconomic policies stamped him as a New Deal progressive—as a man whose only claim to being a conservative stemmed from a selected invocation of state rights to support personal ambition and a virulent racism.[20] Yet those who wish to take southern conservatism seriously must recognize that the widespread political identification of men like Bilbo with the conservative movement exposes grave weaknesses in its theory and politics.

Thoughtful conservatives know that they plunge into difficulty whenever they become aware of themselves as conservatives. The recognition that a world self-consciously experienced may not be worth preserving—that it scorns the virtues conservatives uphold—assaults their deepest feelings and their belief that men ought to take the world, natural and social, as a given. Wilmoore Kendall, beating up, as usual, on Russell Kirk, Clinton Rossiter, and almost every other fellow conservative in sight (not for nothing did a posthumously published book of Kendall's essays appear as *Wilmoore Kendall contra Mundum*) ridiculed those who sought to establish a conservative *Summa*:

In any given time and place Conservatives are those who are defending an established order against those who seek to undermine or transform it . . . I make no sense, that is to say, of calling "Conservative" the man who takes a dim view of his country's established institutions, feels something less than at home with its way of life as it actually lives it, finds it difficult to identify himself with the political and moral principles on which it has acted through its history, dislikes or views with contempt the generality of the kind of people his society produces, and—above all perhaps—dissociates himself from its Founders, or at least holds them at arm's length.[21]

Kendall knew that he had taken slippery ground. Had he been among us in recent years, he surely would have scoffed at the curious attempt of the media to label the residual Stalinists in Russia as conservatives. Tate and Bradford were eventually driven to proclaim themselves "reactionaries," for, as Bradford put it, "reaction is a necessary term in the intellectual context we inhabit late in the twentieth century because merely to conserve is sometimes to perpetuate what is outrageous."[22] Since 1865, southern conservatives have opened themselves to the witticism that Prince Kropotkin laid on Booker T. Washington. Told that American blacks had a conservative leader, Kropotkin wanted to know what on earth they had to conserve.

The tension continues between the southern conservatives' commitment to a culture of folk and feeling, with its resistance to a dialectical mode of discourse, and the political exigencies that demand dialectical responses to the reigning culture of modernism and postmodernism. Tate argued that the twentieth-century South has had to retreat from its historically grounded rhetorical mode of discourse into a dialectical mode, and the penetrating literary studies of Lewis P. Simpson have supported Tate's insight.[23] Weaver, for his part, wrote books that, in effect, called for a new conservative philosophical synthesis.

Tate and Weaver drew a gentle but firm rebuke from Bradford, their respectful intellectual heir. Bradford saw a surrender of principle and a political danger in their retreat from the rhetorical mode. He skillfully demonstrated that Tate and Weaver, with their continued allegiance to "givens" and to T. S. Eliot's "permanent things," made fewer concessions in practice than they recommended in theory.[24] Paraphrasing Tate, Bradford characterized the rhetorical mode as "reasoning from axiomatic or 'assumed' principles," and the dialectical mode as "defined by an interest in first causes and a disposition to seek the truth through refinements of definition or debate."[25]

Yet Bradford opened himself to the criticism he leveled at Tate and Weaver, for he proved no mean dialectician in, for example, his searching criticism of liberal political theory and constitutional interpretation. The dispute mirrored the political and cultural dilemma of those who know that an intellectual conservatism—a conservatism conscious of itself as such—flirts with becoming a contradiction in terms: It must defend itself within an intellectual tradition, and an intellectual tradition implies, in the words of A. James Gregor, "a collection of propositions, a logic" that produces "a coherent and convincing unity."[26]

In many respects, southern conservatism is a variant of transatlantic traditionalism. It expresses a belief in a transcendent order or natural law in society as well as nature, so that political problems are revealed as essentially religious and moral. It frankly accepts variety and mystery in nature and social relations and opposes all attempts to create a secular New World of New Men and New Women. It therefore accepts social stratification as necessary and proper, and it rejects the ideal of a classless or radically egalitarian society, which it regards as a demagogic invitation to tyranny and mass murder. Conservatives cite a long historical record of regimes that have come to power under the banner of radical egalitarianism and then slaughtered people in staggering numbers. We have here an important clue to the current fissures in the Reagan coalition, the mainstream of which celebrates egalitarianism and an upward-and-onward progressivism as the beneficial fruit of a market society.

As a self-conscious movement, southern conservatism has roots in the reaction against the philosophical extravagance of the French Enlightenment and the cruelties that accompanied the French and Industrial Revolutions. Late eighteenth- and early nineteenth-century conservatives recoiled from philosophical materialism and political radicalism—not only from agnosticism and atheism but the liberal theologies that were opening the floodgates to unbelief. Increasingly, they became critical of capitalism's cash-nexus, recognizing it as a revolutionary solvent of social relations, and especially grew fearful of the consequences of radical democracy and egalitarianism. Thus, in political theory, modern southern conservatives have built on the work of their antebellum forebears, most notably John Randolph of Roanoke and John C. Calhoun.

The essentials of this world view were forged by many minds in the Old South. For contrary to the slanders of Ralph Waldo Emerson, Henry Adams, and generations of Yankee historians, the Old South had a vigorous intellectual life, graced by some of the best minds in America. Southerners matched and sometimes overmatched northerners in one discipline after another: political and constitutional theory, political economy, theology, and social and moral philosophy.

Antebellum southern theorists never constituted a monolith, but collectively they did hammer out a world view that has remained central to southern conservative thought. Briefly, they followed the principal figures of the Scottish Enlightenment, believing in an objective, knowable, God-centered universe. They distrusted ideological nostrums and placed their reliance in a human experience that taught men to accommodate to natural law. From that natural law, which comes to us through Christian revelation and the manifestation of God's providence in nature and human history, human beings equip themselves with timeless moral truths that provide the standards for social life.

As nineteenth-century men and women—yes, they had a number of intellectually impressive women in their ranks—southern conservatives tried to reconcile science with religion in their philosophy, but they and their successors have had a hard time.[27] In our own day, when Weaver attacked the atomization and alienation of modern man in market society, he identified the turning point as the defeat of the philosophical realists at the hands of the nominalists in the late Middle Ages. Presumably, Weaver had read Ernst Troeltsch, for he echoed Troeltsch's observation that Occam and the nominalists had "severed the connection between Reason and Revelation" and "intensified psychological self-analysis."[28]

Weaver's view of nominalism as a frontal assault on the universality of ideas and the compatibility of faith and reason led him to take a critical stance toward Renaissance individualism. Although a Protestant, he echoed antebellum southern theorists, who themselves were Protestants, in trying to rein in the implications of the Reformation's "right of private judgment." It is noteworthy that Marshall McLuhan, in a stunning essay written about the same time as *Ideas Have Consequences*, hailed the southern tradition in American literature precisely for its sustained resistance to the conquests of nominalism.[29] But, significantly, Weaver could not explain how the great and indispensable scientific revolution that ensued would have been possible had the philosophical realists prevailed.[30]

Weaver scored more heavily when he charged that the outcome of modern thought has been a denial of all objective truth and that that denial has generated social atomization and personal alienation from God and one's fellow men. But the plaintive cry of southern conservatives for a reaffirmation of religious faith has faltered on their inability to generate, or even advocate, an appropriate theology or metaphysics. Their invocation of a community-based southern piety ("the older religiousness of the South") suffers from a grave defect that threatens to separate the conservative intellectuals from their mass base. For, as many conservatives admit, while piety remains stronger in the South than elsewhere, it is receding and may not prove able to sustain the burden placed upon it.

Still, whatever may go on in New York and the Bay Area, in Dixie and across much of the American heartland a lot of folks, black and white, still attend churches that preach the old-fashioned notion that religious beliefs should have something to do with morals and therefore with politics. Yet, contrary to Yankee propaganda, southerners have always been more tolerant of religious differences than northerners. The slave states sent the first two Jews to the United States Senate and would have provided the first Jew to sit on the United States Supreme Court if Judah Benjamin had accepted the proffered nomination. Jews and Catholics, as they freely acknowledged, found a much warmer reception among the slaveholders of the South than among the propertied classes of the North.[31]

There nonetheless remains a fundamental difference between northern and southern versions of religious tolerance. In the North people are wont to say, "You worship God in your way, and we'll worship Him in *ours*." This delightful formulation says, in effect, that since religion is of little consequence anyway, why argue? In contrast, the southern version, well expressed in an old joke, says: "You worship God in your way, and we'll worship Him in *His*." From the early days of the Republic, when the Baptists led the fight for religious freedom and the separation of church and state, white southerners have done rather well in living together with mutual respect and tolerance for each other's religious views. Always reminding themselves of human frailty, they are perfectly tolerant of some damned fool's right to choose eternal damnation. But they are not about to pretend that they regard another's religion as intrinsically equal to their own.

The churches of the Old South held the line for Christian orthodoxy during many decades of backsliding by their northern counterparts. Unitarianism reigned at Harvard and among the Boston elite. More tellingly, almost everywhere in the North the mainstream churches were steadily abandoning the doctrines of original sin and human depravity for a rosier and more progressive view of God and human nature.[32] After the War for Southern Independence they completed the process, and today we have purportedly mainstream Christian churches that are still reeling under the theological sea change initiated by Friedrich Schleiermacher and fortified by Adolf von Harnack's assault on church dogmatics. We have, that is, churches that tolerate, when they do not encourage, the heresies of Arianism and Socinianism and happily treat other doctrines long thought essential to Christianity as so many metaphors, not to say embarrassments.[33] It is now possible to join some professedly Christian churches without accepting Christ as your savior or even believing in God. This apostasy is now infecting the South, but stiff resistance continues there in churches white and black. Indeed, stiff resistance is appearing in the northern churches as well, and the outcome remains in doubt.

Southern conservatives, even the most secular, do share with other transatlantic traditionalists a theological orientation, however much secularized by individual theorists. John Crowe Ransom's *God without Thunder* is a case in point. Subtitled "An Unorthodox Defense of Orthodoxy," its implicit theology is at best Unitarian and hardly Christian at all. Yet it insists upon adherence to an Old Testament God of Wrath, whose revealed will remains inscrutable and whose commands must be obeyed, no matter how deeply they may offend ordinary human sensibilities. The southern defense of "prejudice" should be evaluated in this context.[34]

"Prejudice," like "discrimination" and "tradition," is a positive word in the southern lexicon, much as it is a dirty word in the liberal lexicon that prevails in academia. It is positive in much the same sense that it was for Burke, who has long been a hero to southern conservatives. It rests upon a belief in an omnipotent God who necessarily can only be approached through a faith that requires community-grounded prejudices and apparently nonscientific modes of discrimination. This viewpoint warns against the unforeseen and often destructive results of social experiments that derive from an appeal to abstract reason—in effect, to ideological constructs. We might recall, for example, that "reason" in the guise of the most advanced scientific thought contributed to the pernicious triumph of racist thought in the nineteenth century. The religiously orthodox Old South, in contradistinction to the religiously liberal Northeast, stood on its prejudice in favor of a literal reading of the Bible's account of the monogenesis of the human race and rejected scientific racism. Generally, this view of prejudice says that a community's historically developed sense of right and wrong should be permitted to defy the latest fashions in reasoned speculation until they are empirically established.[35]

Politically, southern conservatives, like other transatlantic traditionalists, strongly prefer a society of orders based on a hierarchy that recognizes human inequality—that is, inequality of human beings as individuals, not as members of a race. Historically, their viewpoint has often accompanied racism, but it has no necessary connection to it. Southern conservatives have always distrusted the mass politics of liberalism and social democracy and favored deference to duly constituted authority. But unlike many European tra-

ditionalists, they have been republicans, not monarchists or supporters of aristocracy. Hence, they have accepted the principle of the
sovereignty of the people and associated themselves with the democratic insistence that any regime, to claim legitimacy, must rest on
popular support. With Calhoun, they have vigorously defended
"constitutional" democracy against "absolute" or "numerical" democracy—defended representative government against radical
egalitarianism and direct or "participatory" democracy.

Calhoun's effort to provide constitutional foundations for resistance to a Leviathan central government has remained central to
southern conservatism. On the historical point, with all niceties
aside, the Constitution did sanction slave property, as honest antislavery constitutional authorities like Joseph Story and James Kent
sadly admitted.[36] And as they did not admit, the Constitution reserved the larger part of government for the states. If the Constitution had not recognized slavery, the southern states would never
have entered the Union. The Constitution, whatever else may be
said of it, embraced a tacit agreement to have peaceful coexistence
between two social systems based on antagonistic systems of property and attendant moral principles. The Yankee interpretation of
the Constitution prevailed not because it was intellectually superior
but because the North won a test of physical strength. Indeed, it is
remarkable with what ease so many liberal historians declare that
the meaning of the Constitution was settled by the Union victory,
for it would be hard to imagine a clearer example of the doctrine
that might makes right—a doctrine supposedly anathema to liberals.

For all that, slavery had to go—one way or the other. Twice in
American history, state rights became enmeshed in unpalatable
causes—namely, slavery and racial segregation—both of which have
properly been judged enormities and sent down to well-deserved
defeats. Logically, however, the cause of state rights stands without

them. Less obviously, state rights has also been enmeshed in the morally defensible cause of resistance to the concentration of power. In the years ahead we may well have to reconsider traditional southern constitutional doctrine, as the power of government and corporate bureaucracies meets mounting opposition by people in all regions and walks of life. At the least, southern doctrine invites careful reevaluation of the structure, functions, and proper limits of a bureaucratic organization that, contrary to blanket southern-conservative strictures, may on balance be judged efficacious as well as necessary.

To defend a modern republicanism free of demagogy and the manipulation of the masses by self-aggrandizing elites, southern conservatives have focused on the economic substructure of society. For the kind of republic they value depends upon an enlightened citizenry that accepts hierarchy and stratification as natural, necessary, and proper but resists all claims to artificially promoted aristocracies and elites as a threat to individual freedom. Hence, with respect to the relation of the individual to the law and to civic participation, they have taken egalitarian ground. They have even taken the politically majoritarian ground staked out by Wilmoore Kendall, loaded as it is with qualifications that are to their taste. For that matter, they might readily agree with Reinhold Niebuhr that proletarian egalitarianism at least has the virtue of exposing the fraudulent claims to superiority and privilege that accompany aristocratic pretensions. And they surely agree with C. S. Lewis' explanation for his being a democrat:

> I am a democrat because I believe in the Fall of Man. I think most people are democrats for the opposite reason. A great deal of democratic enthusiasm descends from the ideas of people like Rousseau, who believed in democracy because they thought mankind so wise and good that everyone deserved a share in govern-

ment. The real reason for democracy is just the reverse. Mankind is so fallen that no man can be trusted with unchecked power over his fellows. Aristotle said that some people were only fit to be slaves. I do not contradict him. But I reject slavery because I see no men fit to be masters.[37]

Southern conservatives have tried to salvage a core Christian doctrine of equality while trying their best to smash its modern heresies. The significance of their effort emerges from the contrasting yet complementary analyses of the conservative Eric Voegelin and the radical Roberto Mangabeira Unger. Premodern doctrines of equality, Voegelin suggests, were rooted in the matriarchal idea of sons of a common mother and in the patriarchal idea of spiritual sons of the father. Medieval theologians drew upon these ideas to clarify the Christian concept of the spiritual equality of all men. But by the eighteenth century, utilitarians were working out a pleasure-pain calculus determined by an elite that alone could decide just what, in the end, made men happy. Previously, egalitarianism and elitism had proven incompatible within the narrow range of the applicability of all such doctrines, for the stratification of society encouraged egalitarianism among members of the same group. But since then, egalitarianism and elitism have required each other, for the range of applicability has become general. The hopeless quest for an equality of condition among all people has generated ever more insidious manipulation of society by elites that pretend to be other than privileged groups.[38]

Unger, considering late nineteenth- and early twentieth-century Germany, notes that the socialist proletariat depended upon a centralized bureaucracy to serve as a counterweight to local oligarchies and national interest groups: "Nevertheless, centralized bureaucracy restricts democratic participation. And the equal treatment of unequal situations by the judiciary simply confirms, if it does not aggravate their inequality." Unger then observes: "The fundamental dialectic of revolutionary socialist society can be viewed as the conflict between the imperatives of industrial organization and political centralization, on the one side, and the promise of self-regulating community, on the other."[39]

The defenders of slavery grasped the essence of the arguments made by Voegelin and Unger, although they cast it to their own satisfaction. In their view, the abolitionists saw themselves as a divinely inspired elite that had the right to foist its every notion of proper social order on the world. The abolitionists, according to their proslavery adversaries, spoke in the name of egalitarianism, democracy, and universal freedom but championed a society in which new elites would replace old, while the masses, betrayed by illusions, sank into new and more vicious forms of dependency.

Southern conservatives have not easily reconciled their underlying political theory with the democratic instincts of the small businessmen, farmers, and workers to whom they appeal. Neither the Agrarians nor their successors have carefully explored the implications of T. S. Eliot's argument that a hierarchical, Christian social order requires a system of self-perpetuating classes.[40] The spirit of southern republicanism, to say nothing of obvious political exigencies, discourages a confrontation with Eliot's conclusions.

Although southern conservatives have always criticized capitalism severely, they had a much easier time doing so in slavery times than they have had since. In the Old South, outstanding political and intellectual figures denounced capitalism ("the free-labor system") as a brutal, immoral, irresponsible wage-slavery in which the masters of capital exploited and impoverished their workers without assuming personal responsibility for them. They denounced the system for alienating human beings from community life and, indeed, from their own nature. Antebellum southerners read with approbation the harsh critiques of the European socialists, but they insisted that socialism could never succeed because its sentimental view of human nature would lead to despotism. The southern conservatives' preferred solution went far beyond that of most transatlantic traditionalists and called for the restoration of personal servitude for all laboring classes, regardless of race. The spokesmen for the Polish and Hungarian gentry, in contrast, interpreted the American experience as demonstrating the compatibility of democracy with security and property, at least so long as the ruling classes were capable of adjusting to the social relations and ethos of the marketplace.[41] The conservatives of the Old South stood with the socialists in believing that capitalism was entering a period of revolutionary crisis and in predicting its collapse. This belief undergirded the position of both secessionists and antisecessionists, for the leading southern Unionists argued that the impending collapse of capitalism would render slavery safer in the Union than out of it.[42]

The defense of slavery was not simply a defense of property rights or racial dictatorship. That itself is startling. For the North was deeply racist, and prudence might have led proslavery southerners to rest their case on racial grounds. They could not do so for two reasons. First, unlike slaveholders elsewhere, the southerners insisted that any Christian social order must rest on some form of slavery. And second, as honest men and women—and most were honest—they knew that the theoretical foundations for their position justified slavery as a social system and not merely a system of racial control. Thus, Weaver, notwithstanding his repudiation of slavery as an evil, argued that it supported a society ethically superior to that of the North, for "the endeavor to grade men by their moral and intellectual worth may suggest a more sensitive conscience than proscription of individual difference."[43]

The slaveholders invoked the Bible, and their cause might not have prevailed in the deeply religious South if they had not been able to make a strong case that the Bible sanctioned slavery.[44] They invoked the ubiquity of slavery in world history, but, there too, they knew that that historical ubiquity had nothing to do with race. The historical sanction, like the biblical, applied to slavery as a system of human relations regardless of race. And the slaveholders invoked the laws of political economy, which led them to the conclusion that all races required some form of servitude in order to progress.

The political economy of the reigning Manchester School inadvertently provided much of the ammunition for the attack on capitalism. It proved especially powerful because it blended with the theological argument to condemn capitalism as a brutal and immoral system and to exalt slavery as a Christian alternative. The slaveholding elite imbibed political economy in college courses in moral philosophy. And keep in mind that a higher percentage of white southern youth than of northern youth attended college. Educated southerners read Adam Smith, David Ricardo, Thomas Malthus, and Jean-Baptiste Say. They drew their own conclusions from Ricardo's theories of diminishing returns to agriculture, falling rate of profit, and "iron law of wages," as it came to be called, and from Malthus' grim law of population. They concluded that the free-labor system generated wage-slavery and the immizeration of the laboring classes. Indeed, George Tucker of Virginia, perhaps the ablest economist in the United States, predicted the eventual demise of slavery as the wages of free labor fell below the costs of maintaining slaves. In other words, he bluntly argued that capitalists could exploit free laborers more rigorously than slaveholders could exploit slaves.[45]

Southern theorists rejected this projected social cost, and, besides, they did not believe that the laboring classes would quietly take the blow. They predicted revolution, anarchy, and eventual military despotism. After the bloody June Days in Paris in 1848, when the working class rose against the bourgeoisie, they cried, "We told you so," and they were not surprised by Louis Napoleon's subsequent coup d'état. Hence, they increasingly viewed the restoration of some form of personal servitude in Europe as the only safe and Christian solution to the antagonism between capital and labor. By 1861, Henry Timrod, poet laureate of the Confederacy, was celebrating southern slavery as the model of social relations for a new world order in which republican liberty would flourish for the propertied classes and in which security and at least minimal material comfort would be guaranteed to the laboring masses.[46]

The end of slavery destroyed the social relations that nurtured this critique of capitalism. After the War the dominant class made its peace with a transatlantic bourgeoisie it recognized as triumphant. With palpable bad faith, it pretended that its new plantation system based on sharecropping and tenancy effectively continued the paternalistic ethos of the old regime.[47] The collective memory and folkways of the common people, buttressed by the struggle of a few men to keep the upper classes honest, did keep some of that ethos alive during the twentieth century. But the principal result has been dreary, producing, in Bradford's words, "conservative centralizers and egalitarians on every subject but money."[48]

Southern conservatism has always traced the evils of the modern world to the ascendancy of the profit motive and material acquisitiveness; to the conversion of small property based on individual labor into accumulated capital manifested as financial assets; to the centralization and bureaucratization of management; to the extreme specialization of labor and the rise of consumerism; to an idolatrous cult of economic growth and scientific and technological progress; and to the destructive exploitation of nature. Thus, down to our own day, southern conservatives have opposed finance capitalism and have regarded socialism as the logical outcome of the capitalist centralization of economic and state power. Those who doubt the deep anticapitalism of twentieth-century southern conservatives, from Tate to Weaver to Bradford, need only read their many explicit statements.[49]

Today, the larger problem with capitalism haunts people from every part of the political spectrum. With the disintegration of the Soviet Union, the Left has suffered a political and moral Waterloo. Despite considerable internal diversity and dissent, the principal political and ideological organs of the Left have generally suffered from the congenital disease of a utopianism based on the assumption of human goodness or of a morally neutral human nature that must be shaped by education—which often means manipulated by an elite that invokes the rhetoric of egalitarianism and anti-elitism. The Communist movement, for all its faults and theoretical ambiguities, long provided a practical antidote to Marx's own romance with personal liberation as the natural outcome of communist social re-lations. Wherever the radical Left has remained in opposition, it has been able to disguise the split in its ranks between those who at bottom oppose all authority and order and those determined to impose a firmly disciplined alternate social order. Once in power, the radical Left has always reduced its theoretical commitment to personal liberation to lip-service and has settled accounts with its quasi-anarchists and personal liberationists. As everyone surely has noticed, it has settled these accounts rather disagreeably.

The collapse of the socialist system of state ownership of the means of production has tellingly exposed the futility of the ideal of a radically egalitarian society of free and autonomous individuals. Every step of the way, the socialist experience, as well as the perfor-mance of social democracy whenever it has come to power, has generated bureaucratic forms of stratification that have dashed radical-democratic and egalitarian dogmas. However much Marxists, among others, may ridicule Vilfredo Pareto's theory of the "circulation of elites," those elites, like the poor, we always have with us.[50] The more they are denied in theory—the more we are inundated with anti-elitist rhetoric and compelled to proceed on radical-egalitarian premises—the greater the room for irresponsibility and unaccountability in our leaders.

What goes largely unnoticed is that, on much of the American Right, the conservative critique of modernity has largely given way to a free-market liberalism the ideal of which shares much with the radical Left's version of egalitarianism. The traditionalists are entitled to gloat, for they have always regarded socialism and radical democracy as the logical outcome of bourgeois liberalism. The free-market Right professes to believe in a level playing field and an attendant doctrine of equality of opportunity, despite all evidence that neither could ever be realized. The projected hopes are no less an invitation to disillusionment and despair than their counterpart in the Left's chimera of equality of outcome and ultimate condition. And they are just as cruel. The left-wing version of egalitarianism generates the politics of envy and the degrading psychology of victimization.[51] Those who cannot match the performance of others blame sexism, racism, and other forms of social oppression for their personal failures and shortcomings. Their frustration, anger, and irrationality produce effects all the worse since there is often a measure of truth in the complaints.

The right-wing version produces similar effects, perhaps psychologically even more devastating. For it glosses over the measure of truth in the left-wing version and drives people to see personal failures where they are in fact hemmed in by systemic social and economic injustice. And it produces smugness and callousness in the more successful, who feel little or no responsibility to respond, if necessary with some self-sacrifice, to those social and economic injustices which can be corrected by constructive community effort.

The fall of the Confederacy drowned the hopes of southern conservatives for the construction of a viable noncapitalist social order, much as the disintegration of the Soviet Union—all pretenses and wishful thinking aside—has drowned the hopes of socialists.[52] The critique of capitalism has led southern conservatives to the impasse in which the Left now finds itself. World-historic events compel a reassessment of first principles as well as political and social policies.[53]

For those on the Left, a reassessment need not lead to a retreat from a lifelong struggle for social justice against economic exploitation, racism, male supremacy, and the atomization of social life. But that struggle has often blinded leftists to those historic achievements of capitalism upon which any civilized society must build, not the least of which has been an economic performance that has expanded the possibilities for individual freedom and political democracy for enormous numbers of people throughout the world. Many leftists want to forget Marx's materialist premise—and promise—namely, that a socialist society would outproduce its capitalist rival and thereby provide the material foundations for an unprecedented human liberation. The woeful failure of socialism as an economic system has laid bare the delusive nature of the dream.

Socialism's economic debacle cannot readily be ascribed to "Stalinism," although many specific horrors can. The futility of the repeated efforts at economic reform in the absence of an adequate number of market mechanisms shows that more flexible policies could not have enabled the Soviet Union and the socialist bloc to compete with the capitalist countries. And in a world of antagonistic social systems, manifested in national states, failure to prevail in economic competition spelled defeat. For better and worse, capitalism, not socialism, has once again emerged as the world's greatest revolutionary and self-revolutionizing system. In so doing, it has established its claims to being immeasurably more congruent with the human nature depicted by Saint Paul, Saint Augustine, and their Christian successors and manifested throughout human history. But capitalism has not thereby refuted the charge of its being an economic system that undermines the foundations of civilized life by atomizing individuals and that undermines the inspiring concept of citizenship created by the bourgeoisie in its great days. Rather, when considered in the light of the failure of socialism, capitalism today poses anew the challenge to construct a decent social order.

The socialist debacle has exposed the false premises on which the Left has proceeded, but it has done so at a time in which the Right is embracing many of those premises—notably, personal liberation and radical egalitarianism. Hence, the great questions of our time require a simultaneous reassessment of socialist and bourgeois assumptions. For it is hard to believe that, however much we must accept a market economy, we could expect to live as civilized human beings in a society that makes the market the arbiter of our moral, spiritual, and political life.

Thus, southern conservatives and other traditionalists are properly calling for a reexamination of the relation of church to state and of religion to society. They understand that the obstacles include the deep penetration of our mainstream churches by theological as well as political liberals who have manifestly repudiated virtually all of the essentials of historical Christian doctrine and are prepared to defeat the purposes of institutional autonomy by subjecting their churches to prevailing political ideology. As early as the 1930s, Cleanth Brooks, an Episcopalian, reviewed the essentials: "'The Search for God' is all very well for a party of religious explorers; it hardly does for a religion which maintains that it has found Him."

Brooks charged modern Protestantism with replacing the brotherhood of man in God the Father with a secular and politically radical
brotherhood that has become an end in itself. "If the Christian
values are *true*," he asked, "if they are worth adhering to, shall they
determine the civilization; or shall the economic order into which
we drift determine our values by allowing to us whatever values such
an economic order will permit?"[54]

A market society is nonetheless on the march and may well come
to full fruition. Forty years ago, Richard Weaver, in *Ideas Have
Consequences*, plunged into a brave effort to rouse the faithful to
struggle for something better than the moral idiocy he was excori-
ating. Weaver, like Tate before him and Bradford after, never suc-
cumbed to the philistinism of those who, when confronted by long
odds in defense of principles, recite the only prayer they know: "May
God have mercy on me." But Weaver did warn of the ravages of
what he called the "hysterical optimism" of modern man, and he felt
compelled to pose an unpleasant possibility: "Whether man any
longer wants to live in society at all or is willing to accept animal
relationships is a question that must be raised in all seriousness."
Yes, Weaver's question must be raised. And in all seriousness.[55]

To raise that question in all seriousness would require a reevaluation of the limits of democracy and equality in the spirit of the
republican origins of our nation, and it would require a scuttling of
radical individualism and egalitarianism. Political realism, as self-defeating cynicism likes to call itself, teaches that frank talk on such
matters would be politically suicidal. And Americans justifiably do
refuse to defer to an irresponsible political and cultural elite that
maintains a straight face while denying that it is in fact a political
and a cultural elite. But these same Americans demand effective
action from leaders who are willing to assume responsibility and act
boldly when necessary. The history of the Old South and the New

suggests that a people fiercely committed to its own version of a socially responsible individualism can scorn the politics of envy and yield gracefully to those who exercise authority in a manner recognized as legitimate.

Respect for the dignity of the individual, which Christians identify with the irreducible element of divinity in everyman, must be defended at all hazards. The terrible human cost of the socialist experiments ought to have driven that lesson home once and for all. But the perversion of that doctrine into an ignoble dream of personal liberation, whether in its radical-democratic, communist, or free-market form, has proven the most dangerous illusion of our time. The struggle for a humane, just, and responsibly free society will have to begin where the southern conservatives have always insisted it must begin—with the repudiation of that cruel and degrading illusion.

2 ✛

Political and Constitutional Principles

> For it is freedom and not equality that has been the inspiration of Western culture . . . Western civilization has never been a geographical or racial unity. It was born on the shores of the Aegean between the barbarism of continental Europe and the civilized despotism of Asia . . . But this freedom was no lawless individualism like that of the barbarian. It was the fruit of an intensive effort of social discipline and organization . . .
>
> At the roots of the development of Western freedom and Western democracy there lies the medieval idea that men possess rights even against the state and that society is not a totalitarian political unit but a community made up of a complex variety of social organisms, each possessing an autonomous life and its own free institutions.
>
> —Christopher Dawson, *The Judgment of the Nations*

The southern conservatism that crystallized during the early nineteenth century had a counterpart in the northern conservatism of such Federalists and Whigs as Alexander Hamilton, John and John Quincy Adams, Daniel Webster, and Joseph Story. These two types of conservatism—one closely identified with the slaveholders of the

41

South and the other with the commercial bourgeois of New England—had much in common but ultimately proved irreconcilable. The two sides drew their swords over constitutional theory and practical politics, but the root of the quarrel lay in their respective concepts of property.

The constitutional theory and practical politics nonetheless should not be dismissed as a façade for something presumably more important. The different concepts of property encouraged rather than "caused" the different moral visions that informed the constitutional theory and political course of honorable men. Appomattox settled grave specific issues, but it did not end the war over visions of the purposeful life. That war continues in new forms. In our own day the nature and distribution of property, their moral implications, and their attendant economic, social, and political power once again press upon us.

John C. Calhoun and Joseph Story held views that illustrate the comparison and contrast, for they were self-conscious and intellectually first-rate conservatives who shared much in political philosophy and sensibility.[1] Both qualified as constitutional republicans who recognized the inevitability of social stratification and the need for a propertied elite to guide society. Both sought to control rather than arrest "progress" in human affairs. Of the two, Calhoun was the more optimistic and hopeful. Both Calhoun and Story sought to guide the republic away from the excesses of Jacksonian democracy through a return to what they perceived as the conservative political principles of the Founding Fathers and the statesmen of the early republic.

Calhoun and Story early in life seemed optimistic about the promise of political and social science as a steadying force in society and politics, but both ended by worrying that political and social science were lagging well behind the onrush of events ushered in by the

Industrial and French Revolutions. Both, however dubiously, located the source of most human misery in bad government. Both expressed skepticism about attempts to impose American values and practices on other peoples and doubted that American constitutional and republican principles could readily be exported.[2]

Story had noticeably less confidence in popular rule than Calhoun did. Calhoun generally if cautiously supported extension of the suffrage. Story, who bravely began his political career as a Jeffersonian Republican in Federalist Massachusetts, joined John Adams and Daniel Webster at the state constitutional convention in 1820 in opposition to suffrage extension and in support of property qualifications. And unlike Calhoun, Story denied that state legislatures could rightfully instruct United States senators on how to vote on principal issues.[3]

Calhoun shared Story's hostility to direct democracy, but he did not insist, with Story, that the complexities of legal science required a government placed in the hands of those specially trained to the law. Story stressed the singular brevity and ambiguity of the Constitution and the consequent need for careful, scholarly interpretation by experts.[4] Calhoun stressed the basic simplicity of a constitution that said precisely what it meant and was accessible to ordinary citizens. Yet Calhoun's attacks on social as well as political radicalism did not differ essentially from those of Story, who, in 1842, identified the greatest danger of the age as "the tendency to ultraism of all sorts, and in all directions."[5]

Then, too, while Calhoun and Story championed civil liberties, as they respectively understood them, they both placed considerations of public safety above the expansion of individual rights. Historians have been aghast at Calhoun's invocation of the Constitution to support the use of federal power to suppress the abolitionists. But on such matters Story disagreed only on the specific application of federal power, not on the principle. He recanted his early opposition to the Alien and Sedition Acts, defending their constitionality and the necessity for some such measures to rein in demagogic subversion of legitimate authority.[6]

They held similar views on religion and the relation of Christianity to American society. Story was a Unitarian, and Calhoun may well have been. The curious notion has been abroad that Calhoun was a dour and theologically rigid Calvinist. Calhoun was neither dour nor theologically rigid nor a Calvinist. He tended toward a theological liberalism shared by few of his southern contemporaries.[7] Like Story, Calhoun hated religious bigotry and condemned, in particular, the rabid anti-Catholicism expressed most notably in the convent-burning that disgraced the Northeast but not the South. Story courageously denounced those outrages, noting, as Calhoun himself did, that they constituted manifestations of the democratic excesses of the day and conjured up fears that the American republic would suffer the fate described by Gibbon in *The Decline and Fall of the Roman Empire*. James Kent, Story's friend and another pillar of northern judicial conservatism, applauded his stand, also attributing the outrages to the democratic excesses of universal suffrage and a licentious press.[8]

Story spoke out more boldly than Calhoun on the proper relation of Christianity to the republic and the Constitution, but there can be little doubt that Calhoun agreed with his views. Indeed, religious leaders like the Presbyterian Reverend Dr. James Henley Thornwell of South Carolina, whom Calhoun much admired, and the Methodist Bishop George Foster Pierce of Georgia eventually pushed Story's viewpoint to its most radical conclusion by proposing that the Confederacy declare itself a Christian republic. The learned Story issued a painstaking and unanswerable refutation of Jefferson's hopeless attempt to prove that the common law contained no commitment to Christianity. He demonstrated that Christianity lay at the very root of the common law and therefore constituted the guiding spirit of the American republic. Simultaneously, as manifested in his ruling on circuit in the celebrated Girard case in Pennsylvania, Story insisted that a Christian America must respect freedom of religion and require no religious tests for office. Calhoun, Thornwell, and virtually every southern theorist, clerical and lay, agreed with him.[9]

Reviewing these and other matters, we might well wonder that Calhoun and Story did not stand shoulder to shoulder on the great political and constitutional issues of the day. Yet they emerged, even more starkly than John Marshall and John Taylor or Robert Y. Hayne and Daniel Webster, as the principal antagonists in the debate. Story wrote his *Commentaries on the Constitution* in conscious opposition to the doctrines espoused by what he called the Virginia School of St. George Tucker and Thomas Jefferson and to the challenge posed by Calhoun in the South Carolina *Exposition*. Calhoun, for his part, pronounced Story's *Commentaries* "essentially false and dangerous."[10]

In lumping Calhoun, as well as Abel P. Upshur and other southern theorists of the 1830s and 1840s, with Jefferson, Story missed the tension in southern constitutional and political thought between its inheritance of the philosophical liberalism of the Enlightenment and its basic conservatism. That tension emerged forcefully in the thought of Thomas Jefferson and John Taylor of Caroline. Jefferson and Taylor valued Tom Paine's *Rights of Man* especially for its contempt for historical continuity and its insistence that the earth belongs to the living. Jefferson wrote Madison in 1789, "I set out on this ground, which I suppose to be self-evident, 'that the earth belongs in usufruct to the living': that the dead have neither powers nor rights over it."[11]

Taylor ridiculed those who sought wisdom in ancient and medieval models of government and denounced attempts to bind one generation to the political arrangements of another as a mask for tyranny and oppression. He read ancient history as one long story of usurpation and oppression and British history as largely the story of a pseudo-constitutional regime based on class privileges erected by force, fraud, and oppression. Taylor began with the radical-bourgeois premise that "society must be composed of, or created by, individuals, without whom it can neither exist nor act," and reasoned that they could change the society in which they found themselves. Man, he asserted, existed before society, and, therefore, the living should govern the dead.[12]

Thus, Taylor and Jefferson partially separated themselves from John Randolph of Roanoke and succeeding generations of southern conservatives, who scorned Paine and followed Burke. Taylor struggled with little success to deduce his conservative political opinions from philosophically radical premises. Along the way, he assailed not merely illegitimate authority but authority per se, which, he solemnly averred, produces fraud and error and deprives us of conscience.[13]

Southern conservatives honor Taylor but seem embarrassed by his philosophical groundwork and his lapses from logic. Primarily, they admire the specifics of his constitutional polemics and his analysis of the transformation of class relations in England through the triumph of "paper money." Prefiguring Marx, Taylor described the metamorphosis of the old aristocracy into a bourgeoisie that itself constituted a new form of aristocracy.[14] Taylor warned that the new paper aristocracy was replacing the old landed aristocracy and posing a greater danger than the old ever could. For the indirect means by which the bourgeoisie was establishing its hegemony could deceive even a literate public opinion and establish its dominion through new forms of usurpation.[15]

Taylor misunderstood Joseph Story, much as he misunderstood John Adams, his special *bête noire*. Like Adams, the conservative Story devoted much of his life's work to making the Constitution an instrument to render capitalism and capitalists socially responsible. He tried to close the door to unbridled exploitation by big business, and he fought especially hard to tame the laissez-faire mentality associated with Jacksonian democracy. He failed. His project proved as unrealizable as that of his southern critics. Southern conservatives could not replace the social system they increasingly saw as the problem, and northern conservatives could not reform it to the extent they themselves considered adequate.

Northerners and southerners were talking past each other at least as early as 1819. Story poured out his wrath on the southern constitutionalist theorists without noticing how close their political principles were to his own. He made the calamitous error of believing that their doctrines flowed from the radical premises of Taylor and Jefferson. How he, like Daniel Webster and John Quincy Adams, could have thrown John Randolph of Roanoke, among others, into that pot remains a mystery. More important, Story failed to recognize that educated slaveholders, including the politicians, while ritualistically invoking Jefferson every Fourth of July, were steadily abandoning his philosophical principles, if, indeed they had ever shared them.[16]

As if to refute Story's misreading of Calhoun as a latter-day Jefferson, a broadside attack on egalitarianism and radical democracy was emerging in the Old South. In part, Story missed it because he erroneously interpreted southern support for the French Revolution as an adherence to radical principles instead of the political tactic it largely was.[17] Beyond tactical political considerations lay economic prospects. To take one example: When Spain switched sides in the European war, southerners saw an excellent opportunity to seize Spanish lands in North America in an aggressive course that placed them on the side of the French.

Calhoun, in a letter to his remarkable daughter, Anna Maria, laid bare his deepest attitude and that of southern conservatives who preceded and have followed him: "It ought never to be forgotten that *the past is the parent of the present.*"[18] In that context, in 1816 he accepted "equality" as an irreversible tendency in the affairs of men, but he maneuvered to interpret it as consistent with conservative republicanism:

> We have a government of a new order, perfectly distinct from all which has ever preceded it. A government founded on the rights of man, resting not on authority, not on prejudice, not on superstition, but reason. If it succeed, as fondly hoped for by its founders, it will be the commencement of a new era in human affairs. All civilized governments must in the course of time conform to its principles.[19]

Calhoun here invoked more of the rhetoric of the radical Enlightenment than he would in subsequent years. Even so, John Randolph, who distrusted him, applauded the sentiments, confident that Calhoun was defending constitutional republicanism, not democracy. As Randolph saw, Calhoun did not confuse the "dregs of society" with the "body of citizens."[20]

Recognizing the irresistible force of egalitarianism in the modern world, Calhoun spoke as a democrat, carefully distinguishing "constitutional democracy" from "absolute" or "numerical" or "majoritarian" democracy. In the Senate in 1837 he replied sharply to an assertion that the will of the majority is paramount to the authority of the law or the Constitution. Holding up South Carolina as a model, he declared, "Our little State has a constitution that could not stand a day against such doctrines, and yet we glory in it as the best in the Union." He explained, "We call our State a Republic—a Commonwealth, not a democracy; and . . . it is a far more popular Government than if it had been based on the simple principle of the numerical majority." Indeed, to the day he died Calhoun referred to the party generally known as "the Democratic Party" as "the Republican Party."[21]

The logic of slavery dictated acceptance of social stratification and, therefore, hostility to egalitarianism, except in its Christian sense of all men's having an equal faculty for moral choice or, in the words of John Taylor of Caroline, "an equality of moral rights and duties."[22] More than a century and a half later, M. E. Bradford filed his own qualification: "'Equality before the law' is in the American tradition only if we remember how restricted is the scope of the law's authority in most free societies."[23] Educated southerners, as self-proclaimed heirs to medieval chivalry, understood true nobility to rest on personal virtue, concluding that men, therefore, faced each other as equals. This concept was the work not of medieval radicals but of aristocratic reformers who did not need John Ball to teach them to ask: "When Adam delved and Eve span, who was then the gentleman?" Southern gentlemen did not doubt that aristocratic equality implied no social leveling but stood, rather, as akin to the *memento mori* in being a reminder of equality in death.[24]

The broadside attack on egalitarianism, however sensible and indeed necessary to sustain a slave society, ran into trouble. The political realities of a politically democratic polity in which free whites numerically predominated created a conundrum. For, as William Freehling has wryly remarked, the celebration of slavery as the foundation of a superior class of slaveholders had constantly to be preached to enfranchised nonslaveholders.[25] The attack nevertheless proceeded relentlessly, unabashedly defending social stratification among whites and the subordination of women as well as of blacks.

Down to secession, egalitarianism commanded considerable adherence among the southern yeomanry despite frontal assaults and much torturing of doctrine by the slaveholding theorists and politicians. Henry St. George Tucker, a much respected jurist and legal scholar and son of St. George Tucker, provided a good example of the torturing. He explained that in government the authority of some people over others constitutes no violation of equality of rights. For authority results from inequalities of condition, talent, moral qualities, strength, and capacity for acquisition, and is therefore natural. Tucker then denounced agrarian laws and social leveling for depriving men of the right to show their talent. And—of course—only the best men should be raised to office, for only in that way can genuine equality be sustained.[26]

For Henry St. George Tucker, inequality of talent and condition provided no basis for special privileges "among separate classes." Since God had made man in his own image, there could be no religious excuse for the doctrine of inequality. Regrettably, he barely attempted to reply to the numerous challenges on this very point, contenting himself with the assertion: "It is really inconceivable how the notion of a natural inequality of *classes* ever should have found its way into human speculations."[27] Albert Taylor Bledsoe, John C. Calhoun, Thomas Roderick Dew, James H. Hammond, William Harper, James Henley Thornwell, and almost everyone else among the South's most conservative, anti-egalitarian but firmly republican theorists would hardly have disagreed with the underlying thought. They might, however, have regarded so convoluted a defense of equality as less than adequate. Still, planters as well as yeomen all across the South found it almost impossible to surrender the rhetoric, although not necessarily the substance, of the ostensibly Jeffersonian egalitarianism that Tucker passionately defended.

A sympathetic reading might suggest that Henry St. George Tucker and his southern-conservative contemporaries believed southern society to rest upon an equality of aspiration. Regardless of class origins or position, every white man could aspire to be considered a gentleman by dint of his own effort and merit. In this respect southern society had a perpetually frontier quality, which democratized the aspiration to equality. In consequence, southern republicanism recoiled against hereditary status but not against family and class.[28]

From Jefferson's presidency to Jackson's and on to secession, disillusionment with democracy and universal manhood suffrage rose steadily among conservatives of both North and South. Electoral realities forced dissidents to restrict themselves to private or only semipublic expression, but the antidemocratic undercurrent nonetheless built steadily. G. W. Featherstonhaugh reported Calhoun as saying that the federal government had worked well until northern demagogues set universal suffrage and other political contrivances in motion. In the 1850s, James Stirling found that "most intelligent Americans I have met [agree] that the plague of this country is her universal suffrage." Yet he noted that southerners especially mix up practical questions with speculations on the principles of society. Southern principles "smack strongly of the old aristocratic leaven; and though in public politics republican equality is grudgingly admitted, in private the Southerner expresses unmeasured disdain for his Yankee brethren."[29]

Old Jeffersonians like Thomas Cooper and William Branch Giles joined prominent old Federalists and Whigs in the backlash. Cooper, who had been a radical in Britain and then been convicted for violation of the Alien and Sedition Acts, gave up on universal suffrage before he arrived in South Carolina. Giles, speaking at Virginia's constitutional convention in 1829–1830, denounced universal suffrage as the gateway to demoralization and corruption. Among the Whigs, George Badger of North Carolina restrained himself in public but privately expressed disgust and contempt for "modern democracy." A steadily growing number of prominent southerners was declaring democracy itself a failure. Even John Taylor had assailed direct democracy: "Turbulence, instability, injustice, suspicion, ingratitude, and excess of gratitude, are among the evil moral qualities, which this form of government has a tendency to excite." He supported frequent elections because he thought they would limit democracy through the imposition of republican checks.[30]

Calhoun pulled the threads together at the end of his life in his *Disquisition on Government* and *Discourse on the Constitution*, in which he sought to preserve a restricted egalitarianism and minimal democracy within a conservative republican framework. Following Aristotle, he insisted that men are born in society with different talents, capacities, and situations and neither have been nor can be viewed as autonomous individuals. Men, "instead of being born free and equal, are born subject, not only to parental authority, but to the laws and institutions of the country where born and under whose protection they draw their first breath."[31] In the *Discourse* he wrote, "Ours is a democratic, federal republic. It is democratic, in contradistinction to aristocracy and monarchy. It excludes classes, orders, and all artificial distinctions." It is democratic in resting upon "the great cardinal maxim that the people are the source of all power." It is republican because the people do not surrender power; if they did, the government would no longer be democratic. Rather, they delegate power constitutionally. In Hobbesian accents, he declared that sovereignty is indivisible, and, therefore, a sovereignty divided between the states and the federal government could not be sustained.

The people alone are sovereign. The federal and state governments stand in relation to each other with respect not to their functions but to their powers, with each paramount in its own sphere.[32]

Without blushing, Calhoun could speak of the sovereignty and equality of "the people" because his basic concepts had nothing to do with the radical egalitarianism of a Rousseau, much less of a Robespierre, or even of a Jefferson in his more enthusiastic moments. Calhoun normally made careful distinctions, but he sometimes risked ambiguous formulations. He recognized natural rights when it suited him but in such a way as to justify the suspicion that his definition reduced them to one of those abstractions he and his colleagues constantly protested against. To put it another way, he in fact denied the several doctrines of natural rights in vogue at the time. Political rights, he insisted, derive from the collective will of society and are not natural. In an essay on the Dorr rebellion he explained: "When political and not natural rights are the subject, the people, as has been stated, are regarded as constituting a body politic, or State; and not merely as so many individuals. It is only when so regarded, that *they possess any political rights*."[33]

The doctrine of state rights has fared badly since the force of arms that ostensibly settled all questions of principle. Yet Oliver Wendell Holmes, among other luminaries, thought that the South's argument for state rights might well be good constitutional doctrine, however much he dismissed it as a vain political exercise. Similarly, Holmes dismissed the arguments from natural law as irrelevant to the struggle over slavery. All such questions, he insisted, are settled by a test of strength, not by reference to abstractions.[34]

Joseph G. Baldwin, remembered for his witty *Flush Times of Alabama and Mississippi* but forgotten as the author of a shrewd book on American politics, commented on the difficulties of sustaining state rights in a democratic America hell-bent for rapid material gain: "The doctrines of State-Rights," he wrote in *Party Leaders*, "though sometimes ascendant, and seemingly received with favor in calm times, will not always, or even often, prevail, when they come in contact with the impulsive and eager utilitarianism and impatient wishes of the people."[35] As Baldwin did not say, the doctrine of state rights had become enmeshed with the cause of slavery, much as it would later become enmeshed in the cause of racial segregation. It thereby became anathema to a public opinion understandably inclined to equate the doctrine with those unpalatable causes.

Vernon Parrington, a man of the Left who died before the collapse of segregation, observed that the doctrine of state rights "was not an abstract principle but an expression of the psychology of localism created by everyday habit."[36] And he added:

> That the principle of local self-government should have been committed to the cause of slavery, that it was loaded with an incubus certain to alienate the liberalism of the North, may be accounted one of the tragedies of American history. It was disastrous to American democracy, for it removed the last brake on the movement of consolidation, submerging the democratic individualism of the South in an unwieldy mass will, and surrendering the country to the principle of capitalistic exploitation.[37]

The state-rights interpretation of the Constitution has always had numerous supporters in the North. Southerners never ceased to remind their Yankee tormentors that not only state rights but secessionist doctrine had played well in New England well before the Hartford Convention. If anything, regional particularism and state-rights doctrine were stronger in the North than in the South until after the War of 1812. During the 1820s and 1830s, two of the most powerful constitutional defenses of state rights came from Pennsylvanians who graced the Supreme Court of the United States: William Rawle and Henry Baldwin.[38] Rawle was in fact a strong nationalist who only reluctantly concluded that the states had a constitutional right to secede from the Union. The antislavery radicals, more or less deadpan, notoriously invoked state rights to justify their refusal to enforce the Fugitive Slave Law, much to the disgust of Story and Kent, who, being old-fashioned, foolishly thought that constitutional principles ought to count for something. And during the war, northern governors invoked state rights in an effort to combat the centralizing tendencies of the Lincoln administration.[39]

Southerners contended that the Constitution provided a framework for the coexistence of antithetical systems of property, and that all attempts to contain the territorial expansion of slavery constituted a repudiation of a solemn compact. After the war, Alexander Stephens and Jefferson Davis devoted much of their historical accounts to this theme. Both treated slavery as incidental to the struggle over constitutional principles, but both acknowledged that the South entered the Union on the understanding that the North would respect and protect slave property. Davis recalled that Daniel Webster, speaking in Virginia shortly before his death, threw away his own longstanding arguments and acknowledged that the North must enforce the Fugitive Slave Law or repudiate its constitutional compact with the South.[40] Davis might have added that Edward Everett, as governor of Massachusetts in 1837, had spoken for many northern conservatives in acknowledging the Constitution as a compact that required respect for slave property. He, too, admitted that the southern states would never have ratified it without such assurances.[41]

Still, the identification of the South with state-rights doctrine has been fair, for the South was the one region of the country with a social system in which it could be firmly grounded in popular support. This interpretation has generally been called "strict construction," but we may recall Calhoun's outburst that everyone, in good faith and bad, claimed that his particular interpretation conformed strictly to a proper understanding of the letter of the Constitution.[42]

Nationalists bent upon the consolidation of power in the hands of a misnamed "federal" government have long dismissed strict construction and the derivative doctrine of state rights as largely a rationale for slavery and subsequent racial segregation. Yet strict construction and state rights have represented a distinct southern republicanism, which opposed the Leviathan state and determined to concentrate power as close to home as possible. Most northern conservatives, in contrast, looked to the national government to ensure the prevalence of republican principles against democratic excesses.

At the outset, those who interpret the doctrine of state rights as a façade for the defense of slavery face a small problem. Much of the groundwork for the strict-construction interpretation of the Constitution was laid by five outstanding Virginians during the eighteenth century and the early years of the nineteenth. George Mason staunchly opposed national consolidation at the Philadelphia Convention, and, with Patrick Henry, narrowly lost the fight against ratification in Virginia. Jefferson and John Randolph of Roanoke then emerged as leaders in defense of state rights under the Constitution. The theoretical argument was elaborated by St. George Tucker and John Taylor of Caroline. Tucker contributed America's first critical edition of Blackstone's *Commentaries*, which, in its notes and appendixes, educated several generations of Americans on state-rights principles. Taylor offered a point-by-point refutation of the nationalist interpretation of the Constitution in a series of turgid but influential books that armed state-rights advocates for the next half century.

If strict construction and state rights were merely or essentially a façade for the defense of slavery, we need to account for a disturbing and incontrovertible fact. Of the five, only Taylor was proslavery, and even he regarded it as an inherited misfortune to be tolerated, rather than celebrated. Mason and Randolph spoke out against slavery. Tucker wrote the first important plan for emancipation to come out of Virginia. And when the legislature ignored it, he appealed to the American people by including it as an appendix to his edition of Blackstone, which was widely read by those who aspired to the bar and, indeed, by a great many of those who, in the manner of the day, aspired to be proper gentlemen. In the minds of these five men, and to a considerable extent in their political practice, strict construction and state rights had little to do with slavery.

And there are problems on the other side. The supporters of the Constitution, including those who wanted maximum power concentrated in the national government, were strong in the South as well as in the North. How else could we account for ratification in Virginia, the Carolinas, and Georgia and account for the subsequent strength of the Federalist Party—the party of national consolidation—in the South? Not until after the War of 1812 did the Federalist Party disappear in the South as well as in the North. And afterward, nationalists like Henry Clay and even John Quincy Adams had a substantial following among the wealthiest and most powerful planters. Opinion among the slaveholders long remained divided. Many were more worried about the leveling tendencies of their own nonslaveholders than they were about the intentions of their fellow propertyholders in Massachusetts. Many, that is, believed that only a strong and presumably friendly national government could provide security for their property. They pushed ratification and subsequent nationalist policies through their states by arguing that slavery would be better protected under a property-conscious Hamiltonian government than it would be under a Jeffersonian government based on a majoritarian democracy.

Not until the struggle over Missouri—that "fire-bell in the night," as Jefferson called it—did southern opinion swing decisively against the concentration of national power, for not until then did large numbers of southerners begin to think that northern conservatives were in fact unfriendly and unwilling to sustain the social system of the South. In short, both those who advocated and those who opposed strict construction and state rights were committed to the retention of slavery and were quarreling over the best way to provide for it. So strong was the proslavery sentiment in the South that Mason, Tucker, Randolph, and even Jefferson had to bow to public opinion and decide upon their priorities. They chose strict construction, not because they supported slavery but because they saw slavery as a distraction from the central issue, which they defined as popular power versus the domination by big capital inherent in the nationalist program.

Strong voices within the proslavery camp uttered serious reservations about state rights and suggested that the survival of a slave society in the modern world of contending nation-states required a considerable centralization of power in a national government.[43] In the early republic, southern Federalists had championed national power as the best guarantor of their property and security; only slowly did they reverse their judgment. Southern Whigs built much of their power by out-shouting the Democrats in support of state rights, but even their ranks harbored some who were prepared to support considerable federal consolidation.[44]

William Henry Trescot, America's first great diplomatic historian, one of the best brains in the Old South, and an early secessionist, rejected Calhoun's doctrines. No great country could hold its own in the arena of international politics, he warned, unless it could move as a coherent unit. He opposed national consolidation in Washington on grounds of strategy and tactics, not principle, and was prepared to welcome the advent of a consolidated southern republic. State rights, he argued, might protect southern property and institutions in a hostile environment but would prove a fetter to an independent slaveholding South.[45]

Trescot had grounds for his impatience with state-rights doctrine, for, like some other southerners, he had taken the measure of the political course followed by Jefferson, Madison, and Monroe once they assumed power in Washington. Calhoun, to the end of his life, praised Jefferson as the leader of the state-rights cause, but he conceded that the administrations of Jefferson, Madison, and Monroe had dangerously strengthened the national government. Calhoun attributed the backsliding to the genius of Hamilton, whose talent and patriotism, even if misguided, he held in high regard. Hamilton, Calhoun conceded, had done his work well, creating an institutional structure that protected big capital and big government against the best efforts of reformers.[46] Madison, the ablest opponent of the First Bank of the United States, signed the bill to charter the Second. He endorsed the tariff of 1816, and, while doubting the constitutionality of federally sponsored internal improvements, he endorsed the policy and hoped for constitutional sanction through an amendment. Monroe, whom the intransigent Old Republicans had hoped would reverse Madison's course, instead approved sweeping internal improvements and allowed further increases in tariff rates. Arthur Schlesinger, Jr., fairly comments, "The last days of the Virginia dynasty turned into a confession of the impotence of Virginia doctrines."[47]

Calhoun had his own qualms about the efficacy of state rights. Although historians have failed to notice, he retreated from his state-rights doctrine or, rather, transformed it into its opposite by means of a dialectical performance worthy of a neo-Hegelian—which he was not. Like other educated southerners, Calhoun read much ancient history and especially studied Barthold Niebuhr's *History of Rome*. Niebuhr's account of the Tribunate's veto power over aristocratic excesses impressed him as a model for the protection of the rights of the minority against the tyranny of aristocracy, oligarchy, or untamed majority. His view of the Tribunate as the voice of the people inspired his doctrines of concurrent majority and dual presidency.

In the celebrated "Fort Hill Address" of 1831, Calhoun struck a note he would pick up in the *Discourse*. He maintained that social divisions threatened constitutional liberty. Only in their absence could general suffrage be relied upon to solve pressing problems. He followed John Taylor of Caroline in asserting that America lacked naturally constituted social classes, for he refused to describe as classes those who accumulated property, whether slave or bourgeois, through their own efforts in ostensibly fair competition. He recognized as classes only those groups fostered by political favoritism. And like Taylor, he warned that the federal government was creating "artificial" classes through its policies of distributing patronage, privilege, and monopoly. He stressed the deepening sectional divisions, but, if often in muted tones, he the pointed to class relations as the source of those divisions, stressing the unwillingness of many northerners to respect slave property.[48]

The doctrine of concurrent majority led Calhoun to propose a federal government with two presidents to represent, respectively, the slave and free states. Each would have an absolute veto and would thereby be able to prevent a numerical majority from expropriating and oppressing minorities. At no point did Calhoun discuss minorities other than those based upon alternate forms of property: Racial and other minorities of the kind that passionately concern our own age were irrelevant to his analysis, which assumed a community of interest across lines of class, race, and sex.

Calhoun called for adherence to a constitution that respected both bourgeois and slave property. For Calhoun the "sectionalist," only the restoration of that compromise could save the Union and prevent northerners and southerners from becoming two peoples.[49] With these doctrines Calhoun dismissed as no longer practicable Madison's call for a patient effort to establish a new majority when the old has become oppressive.[50]

Calhoun was subsuming state rights under a broader concept. For if states or, more precisely, the people assembled as states were sovereign, why only two concurrent majorities and two presidents? Why not recognize each state as a unit within a structure of concurrent majorities and assign to each its own president? And in fact at the beginning of the century, St. George Tucker, whose work deeply influenced Calhoun's views of the American Constitution, had suggested a collective presidency based on direct state representation. Story had great sport with the anarchy apparent in such a solution. Calhoun, avoiding the trap into which Tucker had fallen, faced the critical issue: the consequences of a radical divergence in property systems and class relations.

If, rather than the several states, "sectionalism" were at stake, why two sections rather than three? Typically, Americans, including Calhoun, spoke of the Northeast, the Northwest, and the South as distinct sections. At the constitutional convention Edmund Randolph, supported by George Mason, suggested a triple presidency, drawing fire from Pierce Butler, who observed that if such a division of executive power were necessary, it would be better for the sections to separate immediately.[51] In 1848, Calhoun wrote that the slavery question would soon embroil the Senate again: "The South will be in the crisis of its fate. If it yields now, all will be lost." In the *Discourse*, he attacked the Northwest Ordinance, which had barred slavery from the Northwest territory and thereby cast a moral opprobrium upon slavery. He proposed a dual presidency, he said, to guarantee the power of concurrent majorities in the slave and free states, considered not as congeries of separate states but as sections based upon discrete social systems and forms of property.[52]

The tension between the doctrine of concurrent majority and that of state rights appeared in the *Discourse*, which expounded both. Had Calhoun had to answer the charge of contradiction, he might have argued that an appeal to a majority in the South implied an appeal to the majorities in states that voluntarily decided to stand together. Calhoun doubtless saw no contradiction, and he continued to defend state rights. The government of the United States, he argued, is federal as well as democratic and is neither national nor a confederate: "It is federal, because it is the government of States united in political union, in contradistinction to a government of individuals socially united; that is, by what is usually called, a social compact." It is the government neither of a single nation nor of a nation-state.[53] But the political question remained. What held the southern states together if not slavery or, in common southern parlance, "our southern institutions"?

Did ratification merge Americans into a single community or nation? Calhoun and other southern theorists answered no. Individuals are connected through their states, and, therefore, the citizen owes his first obedience to his state, although he also owes obedience to the federal government when it exercises the powers specifically assigned to it.[54] Distinguishing between obedience and allegiance, he argued that the people owe their allegiance only to themselves, for they alone retain ultimate sovereignty. The reservation of powers to the states demonstrates that the Founding Fathers had no intention of creating a single nation-state despite the efforts of the so-called Federalists to do just that. Writing at a time when state legislators chose United States senators, Calhoun plausibly insisted that senators represented their states as states—as corporate units—and not as a mass of discrete individuals who lived therein. On these premises Calhoun had no trouble in defending the right of secession.[55]

To sustain this doctrine, southerners had to meet the argument that the Preamble to the Constitution ("We the people of the United States, in order to form a more perfect Union . . .") bound all Americans together in perpetuity within an indivisible nation-state. "We the People," declared Calhoun, meant the people of the ratifying states. The Preamble, he noted, could not list the states as such, for they had not yet ratified it. The reservation of powers to the states shows that the Founding Fathers had no intention of creating a single nation-state. The nationalists at the convention, he added, had tried to establish a consolidated regime and had been rebuffed. Since the state legislatures elected United States senators, Calhoun plausibly argued that the states were acting constitutionally, not as part of a general American people but as discrete entities.[56] Alexander Stephens and Jefferson Davis followed St. George Tucker and Calhoun in insisting that the words of the Preamble to the Constitution, when read in context, clearly meant the people of the several states rather than the United States as a collective entity.[57] And to this day Americans amend the Constitution while assembled discretely in their states and not as a national whole.

The doctrines of concurrent majority and dual presidency, notwithstanding the tension they introduced into the cherished doctrine of state rights, drew considerable support across the South.[58] They had, in fact, been prefigured by Abel Upshur during the debates in Virginia's constitutional convention of 1829–1830. He sought a solution to the problem of sectional representation in Virginia but laid down a principle equally applicable to the Union as a whole. We must, he argued, respect two kinds of majorities:

those of numbers and those of interests. Where a people shared common interests, numerical majorities could serve, but where they did not, as in the sectional divisions created by slaveholding and nonslaveholding interests, a numerical majority could destroy the protection required and deserved by slaveholding property.[59]

The shift in doctrinal focus from state to region implicitly re-opened the question of the extent to which any government should be trusted with power. In 1817, Calhoun, the early nationalist, was calling for a commonsense reading of the Constitution that would give the federal government the power to take action the Constitution did not directly sanction—for example, on internal improvements. His argument prefigured that of Charles Hodge in his debate with James Henley Thornwell over Presbyterian church boards. Like Hodge, the early Calhoun declared that the government remained free to take actions not expressly prohibited by the Constitution.[60] But Calhoun subsequently reversed his position and stood with Thornwell ("the Calhoun of the Church," as he came to be called) in asserting that the government, like the church, may not take action unless expressly directed to do so by the Constitution or, in Thornwell's position on the church, by Scripture. A century later Richard Weaver invoked Calhoun to depict the constitution of any free state as "primarily a *negative* document in the sense that it consists of prohibitions and restraints imposed upon the authority of the state"—that is, of the national government or the several states.[61]

Calhoun favored strong government within prescribed constitutional limits. In this respect he followed John Taylor of Caroline closely, for Taylor had vehemently attacked the notion that government was intrinsically evil, arguing that it had the special function of reining in the evil tendencies in human nature and strengthening the good.[62] Calhoun agreed, as Orestes Brownson, for one, understood. In 1841, Brownson wrote to Calhoun, calling him a spiritual father and supreme teacher of political principles. He thanked Calhoun for having cured him of the notion that government is intrinsically evil and should be despised.[63]

In 1824, Calhoun expressed admiration for the distribution of power between the federal government and the states, but, appealing to the record of the administrations of Jefferson, Madison, and Monroe, he emphasized the need for a strong hand within carefully established limits of constitutional authority, which he understood to mean respect for the prerogatives and integrity of the several states. The issue concerned the scope not the power of government over those relations and institutions that it might properly touch at all. In the *Discourse*, Calhoun praised Hamilton as well as Jefferson, the Federalists as well as the Jeffersonian Republicans. The Federalists and the Republicans, he wrote, had opposite fears: the one of too weak and the other of too strong a government. Calhoun considered such fears unwarranted, for, if the Constitution were adhered to, no destructive quarrels could arise between those who exercised the powers delegated respectively to the federal and state governments. At both levels of government the people remained the sole source of sovereignty and could decide for themselves the extent to which power should check the actions of individuals in the interests of the community.[64]

Calhoun and all but the most Whiggish of conservatives in the Old South nevertheless remained ambiguous, not to say ambivalent, about the proper uses of power at any level of government. They might readily reply to such a charge that even in a well-structured constitutional republic the protection of freedom and social order requires that power be governed by the specific history of the community; by the unexpected problems that arise in each age; and by a strong instinct for the requisites of community survival, tempered by good sense and common decency.

Arguably, those who maintained the state-rights interpretation of the Constitution got the better of the debate, but nothing would be gained by plunging into a point-by-point examination of the issues. The Constitution contained enough ambiguity to invite honest men like Story and Calhoun to disagree, and the debate settled into a contest between mutually exclusive views. All attempts, most notably those of Supreme Court Justice Henry Baldwin, to steer a middle course failed intellectually as well as politically.[65]

No wonder, then, that disagreements over the meaning of the Constitution wracked the southern-rights camp itself. Calhoun failed to convince the leaders of any southern state except South Carolina of the constitutionality of nullification, and even the South Carolinians were seriously divided. Many of those who supported the politics of the nullifiers distanced themselves from the underlying constitutional argument. Even George McDuffie, one of Calhoun's top lieutenants in the political struggle, doubted the constitutional doctrine, as did Langdon Cheves of South Carolina, John Randolph and John Tyler of Virginia, and, subsequently, Jefferson Davis of Mississippi. Similarly, throughout the South the overwhelming support for the right of a state to secede from the Union did not rest on a commonly held theory. Some people believed that the Constitution sanctioned secession, whereas others appealed to the abstract right of revolution against tyranny.

If indeed Hayne and Calhoun did best their adversaries in those historic debates, they did so as legal scholars, not as the practical men of affairs they considered themselves. For like the Anti-Federalists, whose proper place in the southern-conservative pantheon Bradford has well established, they could not adequately reply to the nationalists' main, if extraconstitutional, argument that an aspirant great power required a high level of political centralization.[66] Hamilton, Marshall, and Story were especially clear-eyed in recognizing that the fundamental tendencies of capitalist development in a world of nation-states could not be arrested. Thus, Story began his great scholarly output with seminal studies of commercial law and his *Commentaries on Bailments*, following these with books on conflict of laws, equity, partnerships, and promissory notes and devoting much of the *Commentaries on the Constitution* to economic matters. And thus, at Harvard and other northern law schools commercial law took up an increasingly large part of the curriculum, whereas in the southern law schools the teaching of law continued to emphasize political theory.

The constitutional theorists (Mason, St. George Tucker, Taylor, Calhoun, Upshur, Henry St. George Tucker, Bledsoe, and Stephens) could prevail in most of the battles in the textual and historical criticism of the Constitution, much as the proslavery theologians could prevail in the debate over the biblical sanction for slavery. But they could not refute the fundamental political premise laid down by the Marshall Court and elaborated in Story's *Commentaries*—the premise that the Constitution, to undergird a modern republic, had to facilitate capitalist development.

Northern and southern conservatives argued that economic development must be rendered morally and socially responsible, even if in their strictly economic theory they embraced free trade on the authority of Adam Smith, David Ricardo, and Jean-Baptiste Say. Both expressed alarm over the ravages of the Industrial Revolution and the extreme individualism it was encouraging. But northern conservatives held fast to the older ethos of the commercial *haute bourgeoisie*, hoping that wise statesmanship could tame the savage inclinations of the morally irresponsible industrialists who were rising to power in the American heartland. In their own way, they were recapitulating the story of the Gironde against the Mountain, and, politically, they ended as badly as the Girondists, albeit without suffering the guillotine. The southerners, in contrast, recognized the invincibility of the quasi-Jacobin heartland industrialists who were emerging astride the free-labor system. Unlike northern-conservative reformers, they increasingly condemned the very social system of the North as rotten to the core, and they doubted that it could be reformed adequately.[67]

Conservatives, northern and southern, saw their era as corrupt and appealed to ancient history to ground their interpretation of the cause of the corruption. From the early nineteenth century, Yankees increasingly identified slavery as the cause of the demise of the Roman republic and became convinced that slavery, which supported a class of tyrannical planters in the South, was undermining the American republic. Southerners attributed the glory of Greece and the grandeur of Rome to slavery and insisted that the decline of slavery, not its expansion, had prepared the way for the disintegration of republican freedom and virtue. Similarly, they identified abolitionism as the sum of all the villainies of social and political radicalism—above all, religious heresy and, with it, the agitation for direct democracy, women's rights, free love, socialism, and much else. For them, abolitionism was the natural offspring of the devil-take-the-hindmost free-labor system in which capital rode roughshod over labor and demagogically raised the banner of individual freedom and autonomy to appeal to the worst instincts in human nature. The final irony, as Lewis P. Simpson has shown in his penetrating book *Mind and the American Civil War*, was that, in the end, a triumphant industrial capitalism threw both kinds of conservativism into a common grave.[68]

Despite appearances, northern and southern conservatives did not simply appeal to a common Christian moral standard to decide that slavery was right or wrong. They differed over the very nature of that standard, notwithstanding their agreement that Christian moral principles required a system of private property in which to flourish. The corporatist tendencies in both led to the conclusion that political power had to serve moral ends, with power concentrated in the hands of those who could simultaneously promote material well-being and individual freedom. For both valued Christian freedom, and neither confused it with the personal license they accused the other of promoting.

The confusion arose from their respective views of individualism. Northern conservatives stood closer to southern conservatives than either stood to the liberals and radicals of their day, since conservatives of both stripes focused on the individual freedom of the head of household—the propertied father or husband. Two problems quickly emerged. First, the logic of bourgeois individualism exposed northern conservatives to the blows of liberals who were steadily swinging to the cause of an unrestricted freedom for individuals as persons rather than as heads of households. That the agricultural laborers on northern farms were not generally included among "the people" is another matter, although one that fortified the southerners' view of antislavery northerners as hypocrites.

Second, northerners defined the household as the family, narrowly construed, whereas southerners defined the household to include dependent laborers.[69] The slaveholders meant precisely what they said when they referred, privately as well as publicly, to "our family, white and black." In contrast, the Christian conscience of the northerners drove them inexorably to advocate a Leviathan state as the most reliable protector of the laboring poor. Story wrote, "Let us extend the national authority over the whole extent given by the Constitution"—an extent subject in his eyes to precious few limits.

Story loyally stood by the Constitution in its recognition of slave property despite his deep abhorrence of slavery as an outrage against Christian morals. He believed that the limitless expansion of national authority would weaken southern political power and eventually put an end to slavery in the states. He shocked antislavery opinion by upholding the rights of slaveholders in *Prigg v. Pennsylvania*, but he honestly believed that, by confirming congressional authority over slavery, he had laid the groundwork for the territorial restriction and ultimate extinction of slavery through constitutionally sanctioned national political action.[70]

Story thus confirmed the worst fears that had been haunting southerners from the earliest days of the republic. John Randolph, despite his aversion to slavery, saw every northern attack on it as aimed primarily at the rights of the South and as a gambit to promote the interests of northern capital. He railed against a bill to promote federal support for internal improvements: "If Congress possesses the power to do what is proposed by this bill, they may not only exact a Sedition law—for there is precedent—but they may emancipate every slave in the United States—and with stronger color of reason than they can exercise the power now contended for."[71] Randolph's words, which recalled those of George Mason and others during the constitutional debates, were paraphrased by numerous southerners who, like Thomas Jefferson, regarded the antislavery agitation as a stalking-horse for those determined to create a Leviathan state in the interests of the capitalists.

Twentieth-century southern conservatives inherited a politically volatile legacy, for, despite some remarkably brave efforts, they have found it difficult to speak as frankly as their forebears. Thus, the Agrarians could not easily sustain their own critique of equality and democracy.[72] Their emphasis on the yeomanry created problems, largely sidestepped in *I'll Take My Stand*, that struck back at them a few years later in *Who Owns America?*—their collaborative effort with American and British Distributists.[73] Herbert Agar, whom the Agrarians never much trusted, devoted his introduction to *Who Owns America?* to a celebration of what he called "the American Dream" of individual independence in "an atmosphere of equality" with a "true democracy." To be sure, he identified monopoly capital as the main enemy and renewed the call for a republic based on small property. But he and the other contributors to *Who Owns America?* outdid each other in an egalitarian and democratic rhetoric that almost abandoned the ground staked out by the conservative theorists of the Old South and recaptured by Weaver after the Second World War.

The rhetoric in *Who Owns America?* disguises much. The authors concede little to the substance of radical egalitarianism and majoritarian democracy, and their formulations could be assimilated to the republicanism of Randolph and Calhoun, even if Randolph did defiantly proclaim, "I am an aristocrat. I love liberty and hate equality."[74] But the tactical shift to populist sensibilities was too smart by half. In countering the leveling doctrine of equality of outcome, it veered dangerously close to the doctrine of equality of opportunity, which Weaver and Bradford, like earlier southern conservatives, delighted in shredding as a demagogic swindle.

Weaver and Bradford cogently argued that since the starting point for individuals and groups can never be equal, the illusion of equality of opportunity must result in a campaign for equality of outcome and for the consolidation of state power in the hands of those committed to social leveling. Bradford concluded, "Not religion but the cult of equality is the 'opiate' of the masses in today's world— part of the larger and older passion for uniformity or freedom from distinction," and, therefore, "Equality as a moral or political imperative, pursued as an end in itself—Equality, with the capital 'E'—is the antonym of every legitimate conservative principle."[75]

In *Who Owns America?* the Agrarians risked a capitulation both to those who espouse equality of opportunity and to those who espouse equality of outcome. The Agrarians tried to outdo the liberals in cheering for equality and democracy, while they continued to adhere to the substance of the longstanding conservative critique. Then and since, southern conservatives have run into the problem of who is to bell the cat: How do you convince a people raised on egalitarian and democratic dogmas to defer to duly constituted authority?

And here the Agrarians slid toward demagogy, for their invocation of an egalitarian rhetoric to paper over a basically anti-egalitarian political philosophy pandered to a racist constituency. The substantive attacks on equality of outcome could readily be translated into essentially, if not wholly, an attack on the notion of racial equality and into a call for white unity. As Weaver ruefully admitted, the constitutional, anti-egalitarian, particularist theories of the Old South proved futile after the fall of the Confederacy: "Only the poorly clarified theory of white supremacy was destined to have immediate efficacy."[76] Yet at bottom, the southern-conservative attack on equality logically had nothing to do with race, and the Agrarians could plead in their own defense that, by invoking Christian principles against the pretenses of a science that has often served racist purposes, they were building a back-fire against the most vicious forms of racism. Perhaps. But the political consequences of their juggling act have been deadly.[77]

With an acceptance of "equality" and "democracy" subject to severe qualifications, today's southern conservatives have had to turn directly to questions of political power and its the proper location in the American Union. They uphold the doctrine of state rights as a useful tactic but not at all as a principle. With their deep-seated resistance to ideological nostrums, they acknowledge that no formula could provide a sure guide to the necessary maneuvering through the gray areas of practical politics. Accordingly, Tate, in a letter to Davidson written in 1929, called for "a repudiation of Jefferson and a revised statement of the South Carolina idea," explaining, "We cannot merely fight against centralization; we must envisage a centralization of a different and better kind." We need, he added, *organization and discipline.*[78]

Frank Owsley, the prominent historian who contributed to *I'll Take My Stand*, led the Agrarians in the abandonment of state rights, which he described in *Who Own America?* as "another form of self-government" tactically appropriate in time and place. Earlier, in *State Rights in the Confederacy*, which remains the standard work on its subject, Owsley described the way in which the dogma of state rights undermined the Confederacy's war effort. Autonomous regional governments, not sovereign states, he argued, were necessary for a just and democratic solution to the problems that plagued twentieth-century America.[79]

Southern conservatives today know that the Old South's determination to limit the power of the national government corresponded closely to the social reality of a slave society in which maximum authority had to be placed in the hands of masters under conditions of strict social stratification. They also know that the assertion of the political rights of the individual did not always mesh well with the corporatist tendencies and exigencies of slave property. Thomas Roderick Dew, with special clarity, had seen the tension between those tendencies and exigencies and the principles of the liberal bourgeois theory he much admired. Reflecting on the lessons of Greek history, he issued a stern warning: "Governments of antiquity, no matter of what kind, were considered as possessing every power. There were *no constitutions*, limiting their authority, no rights reserved to individuals. The state was every thing—the individual only became important through the state . . . Ancient governments aspired to the regulation of every thing; they never withheld their action, except through policy."[80]

This very absolutism, Dew suggested, helps to explain the reason that the modern European sacredness of property—the bourgeois concept of "absolute" property—remained unknown to the ancients. He continued:

> [Ancient liberty] consisted principally in the share a man had *in* the government, not freedom *from* its action. *Perfect equality was perfect liberty.* The government might be the most complete despotism on earth, but if each one had his equal share in that despotism, then he had liberty. With the moderns it is different. We regard freedom from personal restraint and security of property as the great essentials of liberty . . . [The ancients] had not yet arrived at that cardinal principle, growing out of feudalism and Christianity, that neither *one,* the *few,* nor the *many* have a right to do what they please; that unanimous millions have no right to do what is unjust; that absolute power is not for frail, mortal man.[81]

Southern conservatives have struggled with a problem that resists solution. The logic of their political philosophy and constitutional principles leads to a program to limit government interference in civil society to a bare minimum. The logic of their commitment to the defense of what are now loosely called "traditional values" in a society in which the market dominates not only the economy but the society itself compels them to consider government interference as the only feasible way to sustain a society in which those values can survive. Hence, they placed great hopes in the Reagan administration; hence, they expressed disappointment with its performance and bitterly denounced its aftermath in the Bush administration.

Bradford separated two questions: What needs to be done to improve society? And what should government do? Government intervention into "the province of society always amounts to something very different from (and often unrelated to) what is originally intended and creates within the servants of the state a desire to find other, larger and larger reasons for their power."[82] Bradford attacked the notion that conservatives should seize the chance to run a strong central government. Neoconservatives and Roman Catholics who appeal to natural law and a godly commonwealth, he warned, commit the grave error of viewing the state as their agent. The Reagan and especially the Bush years, in which conservatives merely fine-tuned the liberal state, produced in Bradford manifestations of a frustration and anger he rarely displayed. In consequence, he hardened his commitment to a general reduction in the power of state as well as federal government.[83] Yet Bradford could also write: "Only men who belong to something are in any durable sense free. And belonging to a society also means citizenship in some kind of commonwealth and submission to some kind of law restrictive of our personal freedom to a degree that goes beyond the mere prevention or punishment of crime."[84]

The regionalism espoused by southern conservatives from the Right and by the late William Appleman Williams from the Left promises no way out, however attractive its appeal to restore "power to the people." Regionalism never got off the ground in the South, and Williams converted few people on the Left. Right-wing and left-wing regionalists have argued that the immense size and diversity of the United States invite a measured decentralization of the economy and polity. They may be right. But they have been unable to identify an adequate social basis for decentralization. Owsley and Davidson fell back on a neo-Beardian argument from regional specialization in specific commodities, which they offered as the only practicable alternative to socialism, fascism, or social corporatism. But while southern conservatives continue to reject the totalitarianism of socialism and fascism as morally unacceptable, they have mounted no critique of such varieties of corporatism as that found in *Rerum Novarum* and embraced by so conservative an economist as Joseph Schumpeter or even of those which may be found in the thought of an assortment of right-wing traditionalists and left-wing critics of state property.[85]

The southern conservatives' lack of attention to Schumpeter has proven especially costly to them. In *Capitalism, Socialism, and Democracy* Schumpeter described socialism as the wave of the future, and he has taken a lot of heat ever since. But his understanding of socialism, on close inspection, was so broad as to encompass much that might more readily be ascribed to social corporatisms that respect private property under conditions of a "socialization" essentially different from that of the radical, and especially Marxist, Left. Rejecting the critiques of Marx and others, Schumpeter argued that capitalism was proving an astounding economic success but was slowly committing suicide by its inability to sustain the social institutions and values, many of them precapitalist, that had made possible the social stability necessary for its economic success.[86]

Southern conservatives, having treated such questions lightly, have not been able to allay the suspicion that their proposed regional governments would recapitulate all the miseries they deplore in a larger national state. For they have wavered in their adherence to the central insight of their antebellum forebears that any government genuinely based on popular consent must rest on a system of broad-based property. I say "wavered" rather than "repudiated" because they have counterposed an alternate system of property to that which produced the centralization of power in the hands of big business and big government, namely, a return to petty-bourgeois property—a solution they must know to be unattainable. Continuing to ignore Trescot's warning, they refuse to see that the only viable solution to moral as well as political and economic degeneracy must come from a struggle to shape the nation-state itself. Their own insight into the relation of property to popular control of government nonetheless remains powerful and worthy of further inquiry.

3 ✛

Property and Power

> Behold, I will send you Elijah the prophet before the
> coming of the great and dreadful day of the Lord.
> And he shall turn the heart of the fathers to the children,
> and the heart of the children to their fathers, lest I come
> and smite the earth with a curse.
>
> —*Malachi* 4:4–5

The conservatives of the Old South believed that the preservation
of a society's spiritual and moral values depends to a significant
extent upon the nature and form of its property. Twentieth-century
southern conservatives have had difficulty in developing this central
insight. They know that a return to precapitalist social relations is
out of the question, and they would not, even if they could, restore
any form of servitude. Their embarrassment over slavery has gone
so far as to make them deny that it constituted the basis of the social
system of the Old South. In their reading, the Old South rested on
the yeomanry, with slavery an encumbrance. Their forebears committed no such error. To the contrary, they located the primary
social manifestations of evil precisely in the system of free labor and
celebrated slavery as an alternative to it.

Tate struggled with this problem. "The peasant," he wrote, "*is*

79

the soil. The Negro slave was a barrier between the ruling class and the soil." Tate also remarked, "The South once had aristocratic rule; the planter class was about one-fifth of the population; but the majority followed its lead."[1] But Tate did not explain what kind of an alternate labor force could have sustained the ruling class of a modern agrarian republic. Antebellum conservatives did not fudge: They accepted the necessity for a mass of propertyless workers at the base of society and therefore called for the restoration of or-ganic—in the immediate context, servile—social relations. Notwith-standing the praise and affection heaped upon the yeomanry and, for that matter, upon the legacy of the Celtic clans, the greater part by far of southern conservatism's political principles derive deci-sively from the gentry and its claims to natural aristocracy.

With the fall of the Confederacy, southern conservatism lost its social moorings—and for the very reasons that the proslavery theo-rists predicted it would. Ever since Appomattox, southern conserva-tives have found themselves in the position that their antebellum forebears taunted northern conservatives for being in: They have been trying to sustain traditional values without having the social relations necessary for their sustenance. As the proslavery theorists predicted, the abolition of slavery opened the floodgates to liberal-ism, including the theological liberalism they especially feared. The reactionary politics of segregation and racism and the stubborn rear-guard action of the common people in their everyday lives have long obscured this process. But southern conservatism, in Weaver's striking phrase, has been at bay since 1865.

The Agrarians called for a return to small and middling property. They denounced corporations for destroying private property and substituting an irresponsible system of managerial and bureaucrati-cally managed collective property. Defending private property as sacrosanct and as the necessary foundation for individual freedom and a republican polity, they condemned corporate centralization for divorcing property from the direct responsibility of those who controlled it.

Weaver, writing in the spirit of eighteenth-century British political theory, described property as "the last metaphysical right." But he quickly added: "The last metaphysical right offers nothing in defense of that kind of property brought into being by finance capitalism. Such property is, on the contrary, a violation of the very notion of *proprietas*. This amendment of the institution to suit the uses of commerce and technology has done more to threaten property than anything else yet conceived." Finance capitalism, according to this view, socializes production and matches socialism's massive concentration of capital. Weaver, who began his political life as a socialist, thereupon eerily echoed Marx's *Capital* and Lenin's *Imperialism: The Highest Stage of Capitalism*. Like the Agrarians before him, he described large corporate property as a stepping stone to state property—to socialism. "Business," he noted, "develops a bureaucracy which can be quite easily merged with that of government. . . . The property we defend as an anchorage, keeps its identity with the individual."[2]

Unfortunately, neither Weaver nor other southern conservatives have examined carefully the extent to which business corporations have actually contributed to the stability of communities and to sustained employment for families and households. For the historical record shows powerful countertendencies to the tendencies Weaver identifies, and close attention to specific changes over time would seem essential to the formulation of a socially responsible economic policy that recognizes the necessity for considerable industrial and financial concentration.[3]

Who Owns America? exposed the chasm between southern conservatism and the free-market liberalism that today calls itself conservative, and it helps explain the southern conservatives' endorsement of Patrick Buchanan's economic protectionism during the 1992 presidential campaign. Agar, in his introduction to the book, spoke for both the Distributists and the Agrarians when he attacked free trade and endorsed government intervention in the economy. The contributors may not have agreed among themselves on all of the specific proposals they advanced as individuals, but they clearly did agree with Agar on principle. Echoing Jefferson, Taylor, and Calhoun, they denounced monopoly as largely a creation of government favoritism. But they retreated from state-rights doctrine and called for an economic and political decentralization that ceded much national power to larger, economically viable regions. Frank Owsley, Lyle Lanier, Donald Davidson, and others advocated strong federal and state intervention to save the family farm and ease the plight of the unemployed. While allowing a wide swath to market forces, they drew upon the corporatist tendency in southern "social bond individualism," which has always had a strong dose of thinly disguised *étatisme*. In consequence, they acknowledged the validity of Calhoun's interpretation of the Constitution but called for drastic constitutional revision to enshrine old principles in a new format.[4]

Since the Second World War southern conservatives have steadily been drawn into a political cul-de-sac, marked most notably by their entrance into the now shaky Reagan coalition in the Republican Party. It was the achievement of William Buckley in ideological work and of Ronald Reagan in party politics to forge a right-wing coalition out of disparate elements that stand at opposite philosophical poles.[5] Southern conservatives know, even if others do not, that Ronald Reagan is essentially a rightwing liberal, indeed a progressive. His optimistic view of human nature should warm the heart of liberal theologians; his celebration of limitless material progress reaches poetic heights; and his devotion to the free market and to finance capitalism could hardly be stronger. In short, his radical individualism and egalitarianism represent much that southern conservatives have always loathed.

Their predicament recalls a Russian peasant saying invoked by Nikita Khrushchev at the United Nations. He taunted the United States for being unwilling to forget the Soviet intervention in Hungary in 1956 or to do anything about it: "The Hungarian question is like a dead rat stuck in the Americans' throat. They can't swallow it, and they can't spit it out." Reaganism—with its rosy view of human nature, its free-market economics, and its holy-crusade rhetoric in foreign policy—constitutes the southern conservatives' very own dead rat.

Southern conservatives rallied to Ronald Reagan for two reasons. First, as a matter of principle, they saw socialism, big government, and the welfare state as the main enemy, and see—or at least originally saw—Reaganism as the best politically available way to fight it. And second, Reagan takes traditionalist ground on social values and stresses family, church, and local community, rather than the state. On these questions, he sounds very much like his southern admirers, much as George Bush tried to do during the presidential campaign of 1992.

But southern conservatives understand the contradiction that neither Ronald Reagan nor George Bush nor even William Buckley has faced squarely. Capitalism has historically been the greatest solvent of traditional social relations. Thus, Marx and Engels praised capitalism and the bourgeoisie precisely for their destructive impact on traditional society and culture. Ronald Reagan has had every right to celebrate capitalism as the greatest revolutionary force in world history, against which, in at least a few important respects, the late and lamented socialist countries looked like the last bastion of cultural conservatism.

At that, Buckley and his associates may well understand much more than they let on. The editors of *National Review* made an extraordinary admission in response to President Bush's embarrassment in the New Hampshire primary. They flayed him for breaking his no-tax pledge and noted that 8 per cent of the voters in the Republican primary wrote in the name of Bill Clinton or Paul Tsongas: "Who were these people but the yuppie baby boomers, fans of low taxes and low morals? Without the absolute guarantee of no new taxes—their tie to the GOP—they were free to seek economic moderates who believe in abortion on demand, feminism, and gay rights. So Bush stands to lose this chunk of the Reagan coalition in November."[6]

This tension has also plagued southern conservatives and their northern traditionalist allies and has reappeared in the rebellious right-wing coalition that rallied to Patrick Buchanan in the Republican presidential primary campaign of 1992. The Buchanan coalition included such disparate groups as traditionalists and free-market libertarians. Together, they defended "traditional values," insisting, with the libertarian Murray Rothbard, that to be a libertarian does not mean to be a libertine. Rothbard's admirable words do not, however, answer the conservatives' fundamental argument that human beings are frail creatures who, in a free market in which morals become a commodity, will more often than not choose to buy filth rather than wholesomeness. Both wings of the coalition continue to oppose big government, although one wing is a good deal more hostile to big business than the other. But while the conservatives resist the federal government, except in military matters, and distrust all interference with private property, they also believe in the sinful nature of man and therefore recognize the need for measured social repression. The libertarians, in contrast, would transform society itself into one grand marketplace for morals and everything else. As disagreements go, people have been known to kill each other over much less.[7]

Patrick Buchanan himself embodies the contradiction. He simultaneously attacked President Bush for abandoning supply-side economics and for resisting protectionist measures against Japan. He blasted the Bush administration for statist interference in the market. Yet only a dreamer could imagine that this Catholic traditionalist would hesitate to resort to federal intervention in the economy once he decided that free-market policies were not working. I do not accuse him of bad faith. I do say that his present stance reflects the ideological disarray of our times and the intellectual incoherence that even our more thoughtful national leaders are contributing to it.

The attempt to translate a "social bond individualism" into selected forms of government intervention in the economy, while opposing federal intervention in the moral life of communities, has proven almost too much to bear. The Agrarians, at the very outset of their movement, moved into politics to defend their communities against the bureaucratic centralization they associated with moral decay. Most of them were poets and literary critics who knew their limitations as political agitators and organizers, but they felt compelled to take a stand on the Scopes trial in Tennessee, which pitted religious fundamentalists against the devotees of science.

Tate, Ransom, Davidson, and their friends defined as the cardinal issue the right of the people, acting through their state legislature, to control and administer instruction in the public schools. During the next few years they unfurled their banner in *I'll Take My Stand* and other scholarly and polemical works. They knew they were walking into the trap of appearing to be enemies of science and rationality, and, in truth, they came close to making themselves ridiculous. But for all that, were they wrong on their main point about popular control of education? If states and localities should not control the moral instruction of their own children, who should? On what grounds? According to whose criteria? Toward what end?

The uncomfortable position in which the Agrarians found themselves exposed the consequences of their acceptance of white supremacy, even as it raised the thorny question of the proper relation of historically grounded communities to government and to private and public institutions as well. A friendly, anonymous, British reviewer of *I'll Take My Stand*, possibly G. K. Chesterton, applauded the Agrarians on most counts but rebuked them sharply for their unsupported assumptions of racial superiority.[8] Davidson, along with no few others, went to his grave in a lamentable resistance to racial integration. In 1947, Louis B. Wright, a southern-conservative historian, offered a sympathetic account of the black struggle for social justice, arguing that white public opinion in the South was responding positively but that a virtually fascist federal intervention was playing into the hands of racist extremists. Some thirty years later, George Rogers, another southern-conservative historian, provided a better-balanced update: "We have affirmative action because the South was too slow in ending segregation and race discrimination (and the South should be ready to accept these criticisms)."[9]

If we take Rogers' point further, we confront the danger in all forms of Burkean conservatism. In principle, Burkeans, southern and other, believe in reform but want it slow, thought-out, careful, and guided by an enlightened political class. But how often does deep structural reform take place that way? Almost always, entrenched interests change course only when subjected to hard blows from outside their ranks. The responsible, humane, decent conservatives of the South did almost nothing to lead their people toward a well-ordered, locally guided integration. They could not do so. For they have always stood for the rights of the community, and their particular communities, which embraced all social classes among whites, were implacably hostile to black demands.

In response to *Brown v. Board of Education*, southern conservatives joined Frank Owsley in upholding community rights against federal intervention. Yet during and after the Great Depression, many had joined Owsley in calling for federal aid to the unemployed and dispossessed. As Bradford explained, the South has always spoken with two voices: It has championed the Whig tradition of earned rights and commitment to "self-realization through liberty and law," and it has "also made Tory noises: in defense of 'peculiar' institutions—spiritual, moral, social, and economic."[10] Southern conservatives, like all sensible people, try to balance two sets of legitimate claims—those of individual freedom and those of community discipline and social order. Their course before and after *Brown v. Board of Education* did not violate principle, but it did, on the specific issue of segregation, lead them into a moral and political quagmire from which they have been extricating themselves only with difficulty. For, in defining their communities, conservatives long spoke as if blacks were an unwelcome foreign presence rather than of the marrow.

A few years ago I dumped all this on a good friend who ranks among the premier southern historians in the country. "Face it," I said, "notwithstanding all the airy incantations to safe methods of change, and notwithstanding your personal hostility to racism, if you folks had remained in power, black people would still be attending segregated public schools and would still be riding in the back of buses." My friend took another swig of Wild Turkey and replied, "Now Gene, if folks like me had actually been in power, there wouldn't have been any public schools and buses, and the problem would never have arisen." I know when I have been smashed in repartee, but, as my friend knows, the problem remains.

One facet of the Agrarians' racial attitudes has not drawn the attention it deserves. Unlike most of their successors, most of the Agrarians took the inferiority of blacks for granted and simply assumed that whites had to exercise power in a biracial society. But the ever-acute Tate, although himself imprisoned by a conviction of black inferiority, imagined a biracial South made up of Caucasians and Chinese instead of Africans and observed that, as everyone surely knew, the Chinese are racially superior to Caucasians. In one stroke Tate dismissed the argument that a racial dictatorship rested on claims to self-anointed racial superiority. He declared that Caucasians would have to do to the racially superior Chinese pretty much what they had been doing to the blacks. For Tate, the important issue concerned not some presumed superiority but the defense of a discrete culture. It reduced to the tribal argument of us against them, for without a large measure of cultural homogeneity no community could expect to survive, much less thrive. Tate woefully underestimated the "southernness" of southern blacks and their contributions to the regional culture, but his theoretical point retains its chilling force.[11]

The racial views of the southern conservatives have led to the oft-heard charge that they are quasi-fascists, a charge wildly popular among those who know nothing about either southern conservatism or fascism. Those who bother to study both honestly must be struck by how little fascism and southern conservatism share.[12] The charge, although patently absurd, may nonetheless profitably be examined. The principal advantage of an examination is that it throws into relief much of what southern conservatism is and is not. For there are a few points at which it does converge with fascism. It is surely noteworthy that Weaver ended his *Southern Tradition at Bay* with a discussion of this convergence. With surprising restraint, however, Weaver did not mention that the points at which southern conservatism and fascism converge are precisely the points at which both converge with Marxism, "African Socialism," and other left-wing ideologies.[13]

Southern conservatives have especially carried on a romance with the land and "the folk," which has nearly done them in—and not merely or even primarily because of the fascist tendency it may encourage. Contrary to dishonest critics, southern conservatives have staunchly opposed fascism and resolutely combatted any such tendency within their own political camp. Among other considerations, they have been inspired by, and have spoken for, small rural propertyholders who have always held themselves aloof from intellectuals of any kind. Conservative intellectuals have always extolled these plain folk precisely for doing so and for thereby sealing themselves off from ideologies, fads, and isms. The Agrarians and their successors have frankly acknowledged this paradox, which, by their own admission, has threatened to relegate them to the political margin and reduce them to the unwelcome role of mere apologists for the more sinister features of southern life. Weaver sensed the trap. Recalling the question posed in Weimar Germany—"What now, little man?"—he wrote, "The Nazi movement has been sponsored by the lower middle class, and all of its so-called innovations are but projections of the middle-class mentality."[14]

From George Mason to John Randolph to Calhoun and on to Weaver and Bradford, every southern conservative of note has recoiled from the tenets that became fundamental to fascism. Southern conservatives might applaud Mussolini's dictum, "He who says 'hierarchy' is committed to a scale of human values. He who says 'a scale of human values' says 'a scale of human responsibilities and duties.' He who says 'hierarchy' says 'discipline.'" And they might applaud Mussolini for his description of hierarchy as a necessity and his call for a struggle against everything, spiritual and material, that undermines it.[15] But southern conservatives have resolutely opposed the substance of Mussolini's proclamation of "*lo stato etico*"—that is, the state understood not merely as a state that acts ethically, but as a central repository of ethics that therefore stands above even the church.[16]

The incompatibility of southern conservatism and fascism emerges with special force in the gulf that separates the fascist demand for state control of all institutions, most notably the schools, and the southern conservatives' tireless insistence that the schools be controlled by local communities.[17] Southern conservatives, as Christians, could only regard all such fascist demands as a declaration of war on their most cherished principles. Could anyone confuse their espousal of "constitutional democracy" with Mussolini's espousal of the doctrine he summarized as "Everything within the state, nothing outside the state, and nothing against the state"?[18]

Giovanni Gentile, Mussolini's favorite fascist philosopher, proudly explained the ramifications of this frankly totalitarian ideology, which he came close to reducing to another crisp slogan: "The personal is political."[19] We have heard that slogan thunder through our political life in recent years, but the thunder has not come from conservatives of any stripe, much less from southern conservatives. Permit me two observations on its wellsprings. First, Gentile's philosophy of Actualism, with its avowedly totalitarian political consequences, has the virtue of being the only logically consistent and intellectually powerful justification for that monstrous slogan of which I am aware. Second, the radical feminists who trumpet the slogan today trumpet it, with a staggering contempt for logic, as antifascist and antitotalitarian. We should, I suppose, be grateful for the bright side. Those who make these Orwellian demands on us rank as Gentile's superiors in at least one respect: Clearly, they have a marvelous sense of humor.

Since the 1930s southerners, conservative and other, have left little doubt about where they stand on fascism. In an essay titled "The South and the Revolution of Nihilism," Weaver accurately noted: "That the South was the first section of the United States to sense an enemy in fascism was indicated not only by the polls of opinion, but also by its ardor in preparing for the fight." Weaver launched into another of his attacks on unbridled capitalism, which he regarded as an invitation to fascist tyranny: "Centralism always points to an alliance between the mass as such and the single leader purporting to be their champion; and, conversely, decentralization leaves the way open for local authority and provides opportunity for individuals to express themselves as such . . . It [the South] understands correctly that the promise of fascism to restore the ancient virtues is counteracted by this process, and that the denial of an ethical basis for the state means the loss of freedom and humanity."[20]

Weaver, sorting out the threads of the southern legacy, expressed displeasure at George Fitzhugh's assault on free society, with "its remarkable foreshadowing of the modern corporate state . . . an outline of the totalitarian state, which substitutes for individual liberty and free competition a fixed hierarchy and state provision for all classes." Weaver misread Fitzhugh and would have done better to invoke Henry Hughes of Mississippi. No matter. His strictures lay bare his hostility to fascism and, more instructively, his hostility to the translation of natural inequality and hierarchy into an excuse for social immobility, the drawing of caste lines, and the state's assumption of power over the whole life of the individual.[21]

The southern conservatives' attitude toward war proves no less revealing. They have not glorified war, despite outbursts of the bloody-mindedness that disgrace people in all political camps whenever they have to justify a particular war. That charge might be leveled at the proslavery wing of Young America and those who have, ever since, shouted their allegiance to egalitarian democracy, although even they might resist the charge as unfair. At the most, southern conservatives have agreed with Freud and Einstein that human nature contains an aggressive instinct that makes perpetual peace unrealizable.[22] Fear and an acceptance of a perceived reality do not constitute glorification and are not incompatible with a commitment to do everything in one's power to settle international affairs amicably. More to the point, the views of southern conservatives must be evaluated in the context of their emphatic protest against total war—against the so-called people's wars that have become the norm during our blood-drenched century.

Thus, they have resisted, albeit not always firmly, holy wars aimed at the imposition of an ideology and way of life on others. Weaver was never more eloquent than in his condemnation of the people of South Carolina for accepting nuclear installations on their soil, the more so for their having done it for economic advantage: "There is no more melancholy spectacle on the American scene than the fact South Carolina, which in former times set the best example of the ideal of chivalry, is now the site of the hydrogen bomb project, which prepares for indiscriminate slaughter on a scale not hitherto contemplated."[23] In contrast, Gentile justified war as necessary to the health of the state, and, in good totalitarian fashion, he laid down a dictum that could only appall southern conservatives. A defeated enemy, he declared as if with an eye on America in 1865, must accept the will of its conqueror as its own.[24]

The attitude toward war also exposes the political gap between the southern conservatives and their preferred mass base, as may be seen in their awkward relation to the religious fundamentalists, with whom they are often confused. Southern conservatives share with other transatlantic traditionalists a theological orientation, however much it is secularized by individual theorists. Yet despite having orthodox Christian prejudices, few if any leading conservatives have believed in biblical inerrancy or have had much stomach for theological rigidity of any kind. The tension may be illustrated by a glance at foreign policy. During the Cold War both groups wanted a hard line against the Soviet Union, but for radically different reasons. For many religious fundamentalists, the Cold War was a holy crusade against a satanic empire and a sign of the coming apocalypse. But most conservatives have distrusted ideological crusades, especially those which remind them of Lincoln, Grant, and Sherman and profess to stand at Armageddon and battle for the Lord.

For these conservatives, the Cold War concerned a massive threat to American national-state interests, albeit a threat ideologically driven. They wanted to lift that threat, not to tell other people how to live. No one, therefore, ought to have been surprised when leading southern conservatives poured out their wrath on President Bush for his intervention in the Persian Gulf, denouncing American policy as imperialist, rapacious, and one more example of Yankee presumption, meddling, greed, and violence.[25]

Opposition to fascism and resistance to ideological holy wars flow from southern conservatives' hostility to the centralization of political and economic power and from their preference for community decisionmaking. But they know that real communities, in contradistinction to those projected by utopian imaginations, must be creatures of the historical evolution of shared experience and faith. Thus, they face a dilemma, for they know perfectly well that the hitherto solid communities of the South, like those of the North, are wilting under rapid demographic and technological change in a new era of intense international competition. For the most part they seek, as do others across the ideological spectrum, to find a way to recreate the essence of their preferred rural and small-town communities in the big cities. How they expect to accomplish this feat without government intervention remains unclear.

The difficulties that southern conservatives are having with economic issues help explain their increasing attempt to influence opinion in the North while they worry about the spread of liberalism in the South. John Shelton Reed, our most perceptive student of white southern folkways, explains:

> [Individualism] has always coexisted with some other "Southern" traits—in particular, those that the South has shared with other "folk cultures," traits that characterize all rural, village, and peasant societies—which is what the South has been in the American context, until very recently: . . . parochialism, fatalism, authoritarianism, ethnocentrism, and categorical resistance to innovation . . .
>
> Alongside the folkish, organic strain in our region's culture, however, there has always been a stubborn, individualist, "I'm as good as you" outlook, a collection of cultural themes that competed with and undermined the demands of prescription, hierarchy, and organic community. The openness of early Southern society, the possibilities for individual mobility, meant that would-be hierarchs of the South had to resort to slavery to keep their retainers in place . . .
>
> The erosion of the folkish South by twentieth-century economic and demographic changes has left the South's version of laissez-faire free to develop relatively unchecked by prescriptive obligations and restraints based on family position, rank, class, or even race. (Sex remains perhaps a different matter.)
>
> A respect for individualism and self-reliance is also increasingly evident in Southerners' economic views . . . Public opinion polls have shown a substantial increase of late in the proportion of Southerners who support "conservative" (that is, laissez-faire) economic policies, along with an increase in those who support "liberal" social policies.[26]

An alternate policy remains implicit in the southern-conservative resistance to Leviathan. Any policy aimed at the strengthening of communities must simultaneously strengthen the autonomy of private and even public institutions. First, historically grounded communities or even new but solid ones require considerable government action of the kind that Owsley advocated during and after the Great Depression. And in fact Owsley's critics were not above attacking him for advocating policies described as "Kremlinesque."[27]

Second, any government, unless rigorously circumscribed, would likely end by imposing the very centralization it is designed to reduce. For typically, proposals to share power—say, between the national and state governments—wind up being formulas to allow the national government to decide all important questions of policy and to allow the states to administer policies handed to them by bureaucracies with agendas that do not necessarily accord with those of the people they are called upon to serve. We are told that he who pays the piper calls the tune. But this line implies that the national bureaucracy is paying the piper, when in fact it is distributing the people's money. Even if the people assume power over their own money, Calhoun's problem would remain with us. For if we define "the people" as the majority of the country at large, with power over everything, then institutional and community autonomy cannot survive. It can survive only if the people restrain themselves in their own collective interest and agree to constitutional sanction for expenditures on causes that lack the support of a national majority.

To illustrate from the condition of our universities:[28] It is argued that if professors or students experience negatively the policies and arrangements of a university, they ought to be able to move to one that is more congenial.[29] But if the oppression experienced by those professors or students stems from the imposition of a national rather than a local consensus, then the reigning attitudes may be expected to reappear in the substituted university and to produce a similar result. The only assurance against such institutional flattening would lie in the university's ability to project and defend autonomous goals and procedures and to assert dissident values. If all were compelled to adhere to standards established in society as a whole, whether established democratically or no, the freedom to move would become a sham. And an appeal to a plethora of communities and institutions within society only brings us back to the same problem.

Specifically, since the Catholic Church, appealing to the revealed word of God, regards homosexuality as a sin, it could not readily countenance homosexuality on its campuses without prostituting itself. More generally, a Catholic university must discriminate in the hiring of its faculty and infuse its curriculum, not merely its theology courses, with its own version of Christian ethics, or it must cease to be Catholic in any respect other than in its claims on government subsidies. To be sure, some Catholic universities do just that—which means only that a good deal of prostitution is taking place. A Catholic university must be allowed to discriminate and to stand on its prejudices. But to be allowed to do so, society must acknowledge the legitimacy of some claims of discrimination and prejudice. It does not follow that any institution should be allowed to discriminate at will. Collective historical experience has prior claims. The United States has paid a terrible price for racism, and nothing should prevent its placing racial discrimination beyond the pale. But it does follow that such strictures should be held to the barest minimum.

It also follows that a democracy imposed upon, say, a Catholic university would threaten institutional autonomy and distinctiveness, especially if the university were prevented from prejudicing the hiring of faculty to guarantee a critical mass of Catholics. At that, anyone who has received the sacrament of confirmation could claim to be a Catholic and yet be ready, as so many are these days, to treat the standards of the Church with contempt. How long would it take for such a faculty, acting democratically, to destroy the very Catholicity of the university? To put it another way, only a strong dose of institutional authority and hierarchy could preserve the distinctiveness essential to the preservation of freedom—and even of democracy, sensibly construed—in the larger society.

Beyond the universities lie the churches themselves. Are we prepared to impose egalitarian and antihierarchical notions upon the episcopal and other noncongregational churches? If so, what becomes of religious freedom? And never mind that liberals could reasonably crow that, even in the Catholic Church, the laity is doing the job for them. Sanity may yet return to the laity, or the laity may be put down by the Pope, who, whatever his faults, gives no sign of being a fool or a marshmallow.

Our institutions, voluntary and not-so-voluntary, are the closest thing we have to the historically evolved communities so dear to the hearts of traditionalists. They require governmental nurturing in a world increasingly dominated by corporate conglomerates that live easily with the cultural radicalism which threatens to bring all institutions and communities under the rule of a nationally numerical but economically powerless majority. The process of political centralization and democratization is strengthening—by no means weakening—an economic centralization that is indifferent to moral considerations.

According to the free marketeer's best-case scenario, a well ordered international economy should be able to deliver affluence to enough Americans to allow us to write off the rest—with or without an occasional crackdown on the lower-class losers in the competitive struggle. Even Francis Fukuyama, the leading exponent of the "end of history" thesis, describes multinational finance capitalism as inherently and indeed proudly amoral and notes that the emerging business and technocratic elite can live happily with a wide array of social policies, just so long as they do not seriously interfere with business. Social and moral questions are beside the point. We may very well be on the threshold of that brave new world of affluent depravity for many people and unspeakable misery for many others which Weaver described as a world of animal relationships. Fukuyama observes: "It should not be surprising that the strength of community life has declined in America. This decline has occurred not *despite* liberal principles, but because of them. This suggests that no fundamental strengthening of community life will be possible unless individuals give back certain of their rights to communities, and accept the return of certain historical forms of intolerance."[30]

The perspectives offered by southern conservatives, which I have hastily sketched, remain alive, if at bay: opposition to finance capitalism and, more broadly, to the attempt to substitute the market for society itself; opposition to the radical individualism that is today sweeping America; support for broad property ownership and a market economy subject to socially determined moral restraints; adherence to a Christian individualism that condemns personal license and demands submission to a moral consensus rooted in elementary piety; and an insistence that every people must develop its own genius, based upon its special history, and must reject siren calls to an internationalism—or rather, a cosmopolitanism—that would eradicate local and national cultures and standards of personal conduct by reducing morals and all else to commodities.

Consider these perspectives in the wake of the collapse of socialism and the astonishing worldwide economic integration that is taking place under the aegis of multinational corporate conglomerates. We are today staring at statistics that project the destruction of much of the young black male population of the United States. If the projection proves accurate, a substantial majority of black males by age twenty-five or so will be dead, in jail, on drugs, effectively uneducated, or unemployable. The faceless makers and shakers of the emerging world economic order neither desire that result nor are conspiring to bring it about. It is just not their problem, any more than the collapse of the family, the inundation of society by drugs, pornography, and sheer filth, or a host of other matters are their problems. Filth, like everything else, is a commodity, and if people choose to buy and sell it, very well. They will thereby create jobs in a burgeoning industry.

The basic problem with the ascendancy of the multinationals is not that they are hierarchical, cruel, or ill intentioned, however much they may be charged on all counts. Rather, it is that they are literally irresponsible. They operate under few if any moral constraints and can, with formal justification, claim not to be responsible for the creeping genocide in America or the savaging of the Third World, or the moral degeneracy of modern life.

Yet if a return to small private property is a will-o'-the-wisp, the substitution of state property for private has everywhere generated terrifying political regimes and, for good measure, economic incompetence. Thus, either we rethink the nature of property itself and devise forms that combine private ownership with a high level of social participation and control, or we decide to live in the world of Richard Weaver's "moral idiots"—a world comfortable for some or even many and brutal beyond description for the rest.

The southern conservatives' critique of capitalism has always existed in severe tension with their distrust of big government. Those who, notwithstanding a renewed fervor for protectionism in foreign trade, condemn the atomizing effects of finance capitalism continue to gag on the government intervention in the economy that, under present international conditions, may well be essential to combat it. In the ideal world of the southern conservatives, we would be our brothers' keepers, but only as individuals or through our families, churches, and local communities. Time has run out for a substantial realization of any such dream. The restoration—or, better, the recasting—of the traditional family would itself require considerable interaction among government, churches, and other private institutions.

Meanwhile, we continue to be inundated with nihilistic assaults on the very notion of legitimate authority and with appeals to a personal liberation that would unleash the worst in all of us. Consider the Critical Legal Studies movement, which embraces many of the best minds on the American Left and unselfishly defends the poor and vulnerable against palpable injustices. Its theorists rail endlessly against "illegitimate authority" but have yet to present their own notion of legitimate authority. We may, if we wish, sneer at southern-conservative calls for piety and respect for natural law— that is, for recognition that there are many things no regime has a right to do to people, no matter how wide and democratically constructed the consensus behind it. But it remains unclear that we have anything to put in their place.

The fashionable calls for ever more participatory democracy, combined with contempt for authority and social discipline, logically ought to lead to a demand for the very decentralization of power that the southern conservatives have always stood for. Unfortunately, decentralization of power often produces local policies other than those which radical democrats want. In consequence, not only do we end up with support for Jacobin centralization, but, since the people cannot be trusted on that level either, we end up with demands that the courts and the bureaucracy—the institutions farthest removed from popular control—legislate for us on such burning issues as abortion and homosexuality. One would think that democrats, especially radical democrats, would want such questions settled directly by the people or their elected representatives.

We face the contradictions and dangers inherent in all political and ideological camps. The reemergence of nationalisms and tribalisms demonstrates the desperate attempt of peoples to take their lives into their own hands in the wake of an unprecedented concentration of power by international economic and cultural elites. Simultaneously, it is unleashing a new wave of barbarism and massive bloodletting. Calhoun's questions are striking back at us. How do we strengthen the political power of states and communities while recognizing the indispensability of the federal government in the solution of vast international as well as national problems? How do we resist a transformation of the market from a necessary center of the economy into a substitute for society itself? How do we recover a sense of national purpose and moral consensus while reinvigorating family and community autonomy?

Southern conservatives as well as Marxists may here appeal to a rich historical experience to sustain their view that the ownership and effective management of property remain essential. If so, then in the revolutionary economic transformation of our time the whole people must acquire not merely a stake in ownership but the ultimate control of management. True, private ownership and the exercise of firm authority in management are essential for economic efficiency as well as the preservation of freedom. But then, the alternative to present arrangements may well reside in the extension of republican political principles to the economy—to a constitutional arrangement that protects private interests, including the right to inherit property, while it respects the ultimate power of the people, acting collectively, to establish proper limits on individual action. At issue here is the challenge to devise property relations that can sustain a "social bond individualism" strong enough to repress both personal license and totalitarian tendencies.

If we need to devise a creative system that combines social and private property ownership and renders it politically responsible; if we need to find ways to strengthen the political power of states and communities while recognizing the indispensability of a strong federal government in the solution of vast problems; if we are not to transform the market as a necessary center of the economy into a substitute for society itself; if we are to recover a sense of national purpose and moral consensus—then southern conservative thought, shorn of its errors and irrationalities, has at least as strong a claim to a respectful hearing as any competing body of doctrine.

A few grim thoughts are nonetheless in order. The southern-conservative intellectuals dare not drift too far from their political base. We saw the results of their being imprisoned by racism during the struggle for racial integration. Recently, in Louisiana they faced a formidable challenge from the latest of those anything-but-conservative politicians who steal their thunder and play to the worst instincts of white people. David Duke may look like a messiah to those dispossessed, alienated, and ignored souls for whom southern conservatives have always tried to speak. Primarily, however, we need fear him as a political John the Baptist who has prepared the way for a more plausible leader without a neo-Nazi past. Should the dark clouds on the international economic horizon thicken, the David Dukes may yet inherit the American earth—the northern earth even more readily than the southern. If so, the intellectual efforts of the southern conservatives are likely to reduce to little more than ill-digested fodder for demagogues who appeal to selected portions of the letter of their teachings while destroying the spirit.

The free marketeers wish no one ill, but their happy dream of a well ordered international economy of morally indifferent affluence for many and misery for those who cannot compete—a dream that constitutes my own private nightmare—is becoming a reality. We may indeed be on the threshold of a brave new world of affluent depravity for a good many people, perhaps even a majority of Americans. If so, I am glad to be too old to have to live with the worst of what is coming.

The current national drift into an ever deepening moral and political paralysis can be arrested. Here, too, the southern experience counsels against gloom and passivity. The people of the South have suffered defeat in war, have seen the collapse of their fondest expectations, and have accepted it all as God's will. However distasteful many of their reactions in time and place, they have struggled bravely against cynicism and despair and have been well served by their trust in God and in their own free will.[31] In their own way they have lived by Romain Rolland's great dictum, "Pessimism of the intellect! Optimism of the will!" As to the prospects for a constructive outcome to the time of troubles in which we live, the more generous and worldly side of the southern tradition offers its own special combination of hope and caution. Robert E. Lee expressed it well shortly before he died. General Lee, then a college president, jotted down these few lines, for what purpose we do not know:

> My experience of men has neither disposed me to think worse of them; nor indisposed me to serve them; nor in spite of failures, which I lament, of errors, which I now see and acknowledge, or of the present state of affairs, do I despair of the future. The march of Providence is so slow, and our desires so impatient, the work of progress is so immense, and our means of aiding it so feeble, the life of humanity is so long, and that of the individual so brief, that we often see only the ebb of the advancing wave, and are thus discouraged. It is history that teaches us to hope.[32]

Notes

Introduction

1. M. E. Bradford, *Remembering Who We Are: Observations of a Southern Conservative* (Athens: University of Georgia Press, 1985), p. xiv.

2. W. H. Auden, quoted in Lillian Feder, *Ancient Myth and Modern Poetry* (Princeton: Princeton University Press, 1971), p. 26; also p. 393. I have followed Feder's admirable book closely on the points here at issue. See especially ch. 1 on her definition of myth, and pp. 393–407 on Tate, Ransom, and Warren. See also Lillian Feder, "Allen Tate's Use of Classical Literature," *Centennial Review* 4 (Winter 1960): 89–114.

3. Feder, *Ancient Myth in Modern Poetry*, p. 28.

4. Ibid., p. 398. For the especially powerful influence of Roman history and literature on the development of southern culture, see M. E. Bradford, "A Teaching for Republicans: Roman History and the Nation's First Identity," in *A Better Guide than Reason: Studies in the American Revolution* (La Salle, Ill.: Sherwood Sugden, 1979), pp. 3–27; and idem, "That Other Republic: *Romanitas* in Southern Literature," in *Generations of the Faithful Heart: On the Literature of the South* (La Salle, Ill.: Sherwood Sugden, 1983), pp. 17–28.

5. John Shelton Reed, "For Dixieland: The Sectionalism of *I'll Take My Stand*," in William C. Havard and Walter Sullivan, eds., *A Band of Prophets: The Vanderbilt Agrarians after Fifty Years* (Baton Rouge: Louisiana State University Press, 1982), pp. 41–64; Henry Timrod, "Ethnogenesis," in *Poems of Henry Timrod, with Memoir and Portrait* (Boston: Houghton Mifflin, 1899), pp. 150–154.

6. M. E. Bradford, "Is the American Experience Conservative?" in *The Reactionary Imperative: Essays Literary and Political* (La Salle, Ill.: Sherwood Sugden, 1990), p. 140.

105

7. See especially "Two Types of American Individualism" and "Two Orators," in *The Southern Essays of Richard Weaver*, ed. George M. Curtis III and James J. Thompson, Jr. (Indianapolis: Liberty Press, 1987), pp. 77–103, 104–133.

8. Bradford, *Better Guide than Reason*, p. 7. Bradford's words echo those of the leading writers of the Old South, most notably Thomas Roderick Dew, on the difference between the view of the individual that prevailed in ancient Rome (and Greece) and that which has prevailed in modern, bourgeois society. See also the discussion of William Faulkner's *The Unvanquished* in Bradford, *Generations of the Faithful Heart*, pp. 29–30.

9. Allen Tate, "Religion and the Old South," *Reactionary Essays on Poetry and Ideas* (New York: Charles Scribner's Sons, 1936), p. 177. This is a revised version of his essay in Twelve Southerners, *I'll Take My Stand: The South and the Agrarian Tradition* (New York: Harper, 1930).

10. My concurring views on the religious dimension of southern slave society can be found in Elizabeth Fox-Genovese and Eugene D. Genovese, "The Religious Ideals of Southern Slave Society," in Numan V. Bartley, *The Evolution of Southern Culture* (Athens: University of Georgia Press, 1988), pp. 14–27; idem, "The Divine Sanction of Social Order: Religious Foundations of the Southern Slaveholders' World View," *Journal of the American Academy of Religion* (Summer 1987): 211–233; idem, "The Social Thought of the Antebellum Southern Theologians," in Winfred B. Moore, Jr., and Joseph F. Tripp, eds., *Looking South: Chapters in the Story of an American Region* (New York: Greenwood Press, 1989), pp. 31–40.

11. Bradford, "Is the American Experience Conservative?" in *Reactionary Imperative*, p. 136. Following a line of thought widespread in the Old South, Bradford speaks of the experience of the South as quintessentially American and the experience of New England as deviant.

12. Allen Tate, "Religion and the Old South," in *Reactionary Essays*, p. 189.

13. See the lines from Goethe's *Faust*, as freely translated by Jaroslav Pelikan in *The Melody of Theology: A Philosophical Dictionary* (Cambridge, Mass.: Harvard University Press, 1988), p. 102.

14. T. S. Eliot, "Tradition and the Individual Talent," in *Selected Essays*, new ed. (New York: Harcourt, Brace and World, 1964), p. 4.

15. For the history of the Agrarian movement and its relation to the Fugitive poets, see Paul Conkin, *The Southern Agrarians* (Knoxville: University of Tennessee Press, 1988).

16. See especially Richard Weaver, *Ideas Have Consequences* (Chicago: University of Chicago Press, 1948); and idem, *Visions of Order: The Cultural Crisis of Our Time* (Baton Rouge: Louisiana State University Press, 1964).

17. For examples of the southern conservatives' positive assessments of the black contribution to southern culture and their increasing efforts to purge their movement of the vestiges of racism see, in general, the work of Robert Penn Warren and John Shelton Reed and such specific items as Charles P. Roland, "The South and the Agrarians," in Havard and Sullivan, eds., *Band of Prophets*, pp. 19–39; Bradford, *A Better Guide than Reason*, p. 41; George C. Rogers, Jr., "A Southern Political Tradition," in Fifteen Southerners, *Why the South Will Survive* (Athens: University of Georgia Press, 1981), p. 89.

18. Samuel Francis, *Beautiful Losers: Essays in the Failure of American Conservatism* (Columbia: University of Missouri Press, 1993), which appeared after this book had gone to press, should be consulted by those who wish to understand the political difficulties that currently plague the traditionalist Right, especially its southern-conservative wing.

1. Lineaments of the Southern Tradition

1. Richard Weaver, *Ideas Have Consequences* (Chicago: University of Chicago Press, 1948), pp. 1–2.

2. Lewis P. Simpson, "The Southern Republic of Letters and *I'll Take My Stand*," in William C. Havard and Walter Sullivan, eds., *A Band of Prophets: The Vanderbilt Agrarians after Fifty Years* (Baton Rouge: Louisiana State University Press, 1982), p. 86; Robert Wooster Stallman, "The New Criticism and the Southern Critics," in Allen Tate, ed., *Southern Vanguard: The John Peale Bishop Memorial Volume* (New York: Prentice-Hall, 1947), p. 28; Richard M. Weaver, *The Southern Tradition at Bay* (Washington: Regnery Gateway, 1989), pp. 14–15.

3. Paul Conkin, *The Southern Agrarians* (Knoxville: University of Tennessee Press, 1988), pp. 87–88; Twelve Southerners, *I'll Take My Stand: The South and the Agrarian Tradition* (New York: Harper, 1930); Herbert Agar and Allen Tate, eds., *Who Owns America? A New Declaration of Independence* (Boston: Houghton Mifflin, 1936); "Discussion," in Havard and Sullivan, eds., *Band of Prophets*, pp. 159–190.

4. Allen Tate, "Faulkner, *Sanctuary* and the Southern Myth," in *Memoirs and Opinions, 1926–1974* (Chicago: Swallow Press, 1975), pp. 144–154; T. S. Eliot,

Christianity and Culture: The Idea of a Christian Society and Notes toward a Definition of Culture (New York: Harcourt, Brace and World, 1960), p. 41.

5. For a good, brief statement on this difference, see Ernst Troeltsch, *The Social Teachings of the Christian Churches*, trans. Olive Wyon, 2 vols. (London: Allen and Unwin, 1950), vol. 2, p. 1005.

6. Saint Augustine, *The City of God*, trans. Marcus Dods (New York: Modern Library, 1950), p. 477; Leo XII, "Rerum Novarum," no. 9, in Joseph Husslein, *The Christian Social Manifesto: An Interpretive Study of the Encyclicals "Rerum Novarum" and "Quadregesimo Anno" of Pope Leo XIII and Pope Pius XI* (New York: Bruce Publishing, 1931), and see pp. 119, 151 of Husslein's text; John Paul II, *Dominum et Vivificantem* (Washington: U.S. Catholic Conference, 1986), no. 38; *Centesimus Annus* (Washington: U.S. Catholic Conference, 1981), nos. 17, 36, 42. Between these encyclicals see especially Pius XI, *Quadregesimo Anno*, in Husserlein, *Christian Social Manifesto*, pp. 284–323.

7. Karl Marx, *Capital*, 3 vols. (Moscow: Foreign Languages Publishing House, 1961–1962), vol. 1, pp. 71–83.

8. James Henley Thornwell, as quoted by Morton H. Smith, *Studies in Southern Presbyterian Theology* (Philipsburg, N.J.: Presbyterian and Reformed Publishing, 1987), p. 153.

9. Karl Barth, "The Christian Community and the Civil Community," in *Karl Barth: Theologian of Freedom*, ed. Clifford Green (Minneapolis: Fortress Press, 1991), p. 285.

10. Simpson, "The Southern Republic of Letters and *I'll Take My Stand*," in Havard and Sullivan, eds., *Band of Prophets*, p. 87. John Lukacs develops the theme of the spiritualization of matter in *Historical Consciousness, or the Remembered Past*, rev. ed. (New York: Schocken, 1985); see also John Lukacs, *The End of the Twentieth Century and the End of the Modern Age* (New York: Ticknor and Fields, 1993).

11. Donald Davidson, *Southern Writers in the Modern World* (Athens: University of Georgia Press, 1958), p. 45.

12. Richard M. Weaver, "Agrarianism in Exile," in *The Southern Essays of Richard Weaver*, ed. George M. Curtis III and James J. Thompson, Jr. (Indianapolis: Liberty Press, 1987), pp. 29–49; see also John Crowe Ransom, "What Does the South Want?" in Agar and Tate, eds., *Who Owns America?* pp. 180–181.

13. John Shelton Reed, "For Dixieland: The Sectionalism of *I'll Take My Stand*," in Havard and Sullivan, eds., *Band of Prophets*, pp. 41–64.

14. M. E. Bradford, *Remembering Who We Are: Observations of a Southern Conservative* (Athens: University of Georgia Press, 1985), p. xiv.

15. Davidson, *Southern Writers in the Modern World*, pp. 29–30.

16. Tate, "The New Provincialism," quoted in Davidson, *Southern Writers in the Modern World*, p. 59.

17. John Shelton Reed, "The Same Old Stand," in Fifteen Southerners, *Why the South Will Survive* (Athens: University of Georgia Press, 1981), p. 14.

18. Clyde N. Wilson, "Introduction" to Fifteen Southerners, *Why the South Will Survive*, p. 3.

19. Russell Kirk, *The Conservative Mind in America: From Burke to Eliot*, 7th ed. (Chicago: Regnery Books, 1986), p. 20.

20. For a blistering attack on Bilbo by a prominent conservative community and political leader, see William Alexander Percy, *Lanterns on the Levee: Recollections of a Planter's Son* (Baton Rouge: Louisiana State University Press, 1973).

21. Wilmoore Kendall, *The Conservative Affirmation in America* (Chicago: Gateway Editions, 1985), p. xxv.

22. M. E. Bradford, *The Reactionary Imperative: Essays Literary and Political* (Peru, Ill.: Sherwood Sugden, 1990), Preface, pages unnumbered.

23. Tate, "A Southern Mode of the Imagination," in *Essays of Four Decades* (Chicago: Swallow Press, 1968), pp. 577–592; Lewis P. Simpson, *The Dispossessed Garden: Pastoral and History in Southern Literature* (Athens: University of Georgia Press, 1975), especially pp. 78–100.

24. M. E. Bradford, "Rumors of Mortality: An Introduction to Allen Tate," in *Generations of the Faithful Heart: On the Literature of the South* (La Salle, Ill.: Sherwood Sugden, 1983), pp. 73–113.

25. Bradford, "Where We Were Born and Raised," *Reactionary Imperative*, p. 115.

26. A. James Gregor, *The Ideology of Fascism: The Rationale of Totalitarianism* (New York: Free Press, 1969), p. 37.

27. Most notably among women who published: Augusta Jane Evans, novelist, and Louisa Susanna McCord, economist, social critic, and poet.

28. Troeltsch, *Social Teachings of the Christian Churches*, vol. 2, p. 464.

29. Herbert Marshall McLuhan, "The Southern Quality," in Allen Tate, ed., *Southern Vanguard*, pp. 107–108. For Tate's similar views, see Mark Malvasi, "Risen from the Bloody Sod: Recovering the Southern Tradition" (diss., University of Rochester, 1991), pp. 137–138.

30. Writing at about the same time in Germany, Carl Schmitt, among other

continental conservatives, took a similar view of nominalism and struggled to turn back the charge that antinominalism led into a cul-de-sac. See Paul A. Gottfried, *Carl Schmitt: Politics and Theory* (New York: Greenwood Press, 1990), p. 49.

31. The rampant anti-Catholicism and anti-Semitism in the abolitionist movement await their historian, although Louis Filler, in a book clearly sympathetic to the antislavery cause, posed the question sharply. See *The Crusade against Slavery: Friends, Foes, and Reforms, 1820–1860* (Algonac, Mich.: Reference Publications, 1986), pp. 183–185.

32. See especially Daniel Walker Howe, *The Unitarian Conscience: Harvard Moral Philosophy, 1805–1861* (Middletown, Conn.: Wesleyan University Press, 1988); H. Shelton Smith, *Changing Conceptions of Original Sin: A Study in American Theology since 1750* (New York: Charles Scribner's Sons, 1955); James Turner, *Without God, without Creed: The Origins of Unbelief in America* (Baltimore: Johns Hopkins University Press, 1985).

33. For a learned and sympathetic treatment of this sea change, see Jaroslav Pelikan, *The Christian Tradition: A History of the Development of Doctrine*, 5 vols. (Chicago: University of Chicago Press, 1989), especially vols. 1 and 5; and idem, *Jesus through the Centuries: His Place in the History of Culture* (New Haven: Yale University Press, 1985).

34. John Crowe Ransom, *God without Thunder: An Unorthodox Defense of Orthodoxy* (New York: Harcourt, Brace, 1930); and see the critical assessment by Malvasi, "Risen from the Bloody Sod," pp. 317–354. Bradford, Weaver, and other southern conservatives have criticized Christian fundamentalism in passing comments in their books. I shall return to some of the political implications in Chapter 3.

35. Thus, scientific racism flourished at Harvard and other leading northern colleges but was shut out of southern colleges before the war. Scientific racists like Josiah Nott of Mobile came under sustained and heavy fire from the antebellum clergy. Southern thought was itself deeply itself racist, but it rested on theories of cultural inferiority that left open the possibility of the slow advancement of the black race to the level of the white.

36. From his early years in politics in Massachusetts, Story denounced slavery, not merely the slave trade, as "repugnant" to natural rights and justice, and throughout his career he opposed any extension of slave territory. See especially Joseph Story, "Piracy and the Slave Trade," in *The Miscellaneous Writings of Joseph Story*, ed. W. W. Story (Boston: Charles C. Little and James Brown, 1852), p. 136. But he dutifully accepted the constitutionality of slavery and the

fugitive slave law, as highlighted by his famous decision in *Prigg v. Pennsylvania*. James Kent ran the same course, denouncing slavery as an enormity and a violation of Christianity and yet supporting Story on *Prigg*. See James Kent, *Commentaries on American Law*, 4 vols. 2nd ed. (New York: O. Halstead, 1832), vol. 1, pp. 8, 191–200; vol. 2, pp. 249–258.

37. Reinhold Niebuhr, *Moral Man in Immoral Society: A Study in Ethics and Politics* (New York: Charles Scribner's Sons, 1932), p. 159. For Wilmoore Kendall's defense of majoritarianism, see any of his books but especially *Wilmoore Kendall Contra Mundum*, ed. Nellie D. Kendall (New Rochelle, N.Y.: Arlington House, 1971); and C. S. Lewis, *Present Concerns*, ed. Walter Hooper (New York: Harcourt, Brace, Jovanovich, 1986), p. 17.

38. See especially Eric Voegelin, *From Enlightenment to Revolution* (Durham: Duke University Press, 1975), pp. 71–72.

39. Roberto Mangabeira Unger, *Law in Modern Society: Toward a Criticism of Social Theory* (New York: Free Press, 1976), pp. 191, 233.

40. T. S. Eliot, "Notes towards a Definition of Culture," in *Christianity and Culture* (New York: Harcourt, Brace and World, 1940), pp. 114–117, 134.

41. Joseph Rothschild, "Introduction" to Béla K. Király and George Barany, eds., *East Central European Perceptions of Early America* (Lisse, The Netherlands: Peter De Ridder Press, 1977), p. 15.

42. George Fitzhugh, here at least, provides a typical case. An extreme advocate of slavery, he remained a staunch Unionist until the final hour. Virtually every important Unionist in the plantation states and many—probably a large majority—of the Unionists in the border states staunchly supported slavery and argued that secession and war could only result in a general emancipation.

43. Weaver, *Southern Tradition at Bay*, p. 19.

44. For an elaboration, see the references I cite in my introduction to this book, p. 106, n. 10.

45. Paul Conkin writes of Tucker's pro-emancipation economic theory, "Surely no one ever offered a gloomier reason for eventual emancipation." *Prophets of Prosperity: America's First Political Economists* (Bloomington: Indiana University Press, 1980), p. 161. For the relation of political economy to the proslavery argument, see Eugene D. Genovese and Elizabeth Fox-Genovese, "Slavery, Economic Development, and the Law: The Dilemma of Southern Political Economists, 1790–1860," *Washington and Lee Law Review* 41 (Winter 1984): 1–29.

46. For an elaboration, see Eugene D. Genovese, *The Slaveholders' Dilemma:*

Freedom and Progress in Southern Conservative Thought, 1820–1860 (Columbia: University of South Carolina Press, 1991).

47. See, e.g., Louis A. Ferleger and Jay R. Mandle, *A New Mandate: Democratic Choices for a Prosperous Economy* (Columbia: University of Missouri Press, 1994); and "Sharecropping Contracts in the Late Nineteenth Century South," *Agricultural History* 67 (Summer 1993): 31–46.

48. M. E. Bradford, "Introduction" to Andrew Lytle, *From Babylon to Eden: The Social and Political Essays of Andrew Lytle*, ed. Bradford (New York: Knopf, 1949), p. xxi. See also Percy, *Lanterns on the Levee*; and V. O. Key, *Southern Politics in State and Nation* (New York: Knopf, 1949), pp. 302–310.

49. John Shelton Reed notes that the Agrarians' hostility to capitalism was similar to that of the New Left of the 1960s: "For Dixieland: The Sectionalism of *I'll Take My Stand*," in Havard and Sullivan, eds., *Band of Prophets*, p. 43.

50. The circulation of elites and classes is a principal theme of Vilfredo Pareto, *The Mind and Society: A Treatise on General Sociology*, ed. Arthur Livingston, trans. Andrew Bongiorno and Arthur Livingston, 4 vols. in 2 (New York: Dover, 1963), especially vols. 1 and 4.

51. "'The whole secret,' broke off Judge Henry, 'lies in the way you treat people. As soon as you treat men as your brothers, they are ready to acknowledge you—if you deserve it—as their superior.'" Owen Wister, *The Virginian: A Horseman of the Plains* (New York: Signet Classics, 1979), p. 143.

52. A skeptical friend sniffs at the suggestion that the socialist hopes of the Left have been drowned in the wake of the collapse of the socialist countries: "Would that it were so. It merely frees them to hope without the embarrassment of existing examples." He may be right, but I pin my own slim hopes for the Left on a resurgence of good faith and good sense.

53. In speaking of "the Left," I am well aware that a substantial minority within it—perhaps even a majority, for all anyone knows—have taken the measure of its current course and are appalled. Many tendencies exist within the Left, but only the radical liberationists have financial and organizational resources—in no small part because they command the support of foundations, the media, and the academic Establishment. Long before the collapse of the Soviet Union, honest and able leftists like Louis Ferleger and Jay Mandle argued that a socialist economy would fail unless it embraced a variety of market mechanisms. They were proven right but remain virtually shut out of the radical press. Throughout the country leftists on campuses express revulsion, not to say horror, at the ravages of "political correctness," but, with few exceptions, they maintain a public silence. When a few years ago, in the liberal *New Republic*,

I remarked on the Left's disgraceful behavior on the campuses, I expected little more than vituperation from leftists. I got plenty of that. But to my surprise and delight, I was deluged by letters and phone calls of agreement and support from New Leftists as well as Old. Alas, the communications were private and, therefore, of personal but not political significance. In politics, as in much else, the old ad for Winston cigarettes spoke the truth: "It's what's up front that counts."

54. Brooks, "A Plea to the Protestant Churches," in Agar and Tate, eds., *Who Owns America?* pp. 327–330.

55. Weaver, *Ideas Have Consequences*, p. 11.

2. Political and Constitutional Principles

1. On Calhoun, see especially Charles Wiltse, *John C. Calhoun*, 3 vols. (Indianapolis: Bobbs-Merrrrill, 1944–1951); Margaret Coit, *John C. Calhoun: American Portrait* (Boston: Houghton Mifflin, 1950). For Calhoun's political theory, see especially Clyde Wilson's introductory remarks and notes to *The Papers of John C. Calhoun*, 21 vols. to date (Columbia: University of South Carolina Press, 1959–); and Clyde Wilson, ed., *The Essential Calhoun: Selections from Writings, Speeches, and Letters* (New Brunswick, N.J.: Transaction Publishers, 1991). On Story, see especially James McLellan, *Joseph Story and the American Constitution: A Study in Political and Legal Thought, with Selected Writings* (Norman: University of Oklahoma Press, 1971); supplemented by Gerald T. Dunne, *Justice Joseph Story and the Rise of the Supreme Court* (New York: Simon and Schuster, 1970); and R. Kent Newmyer, *Supreme Court Justice Joseph Story: Statesman of the Old Republic* (Chapel Hill: University of North Carolina Press, 1985). As fine as the work of these and other scholars has been, there is no substitute for a careful reading of the voluminous writings, letters, and speeches in *The Papers of John C. Calhoun*, supplemented by *The Works of John C. Calhoun*, ed. Richard K. Crallé, 6 vols. (New York: Appleton, 1851–1856); Joseph Story, *Life and Letters of Joseph Story*, ed. William W. Story, 2 vols. (Boston: Charles C. Little and James Brown, 1851); Story, *The Miscellaneous Writings of Joseph Story*, ed. W. W. Story (Boston: Charles C. Little and James Brown, [1852]); idem, *Commentaries on the Constitution of the United States*, ed. W. W. Story, 2 vols., 2nd ed. (Boston: Charles C. Little and James Brown, 1851).

2. For Story's early views, see "Course of Legal Study" (1817) and "Characteristics of the Age" (1826); for his later pessimism, see "The Science of

Government" (1834). All are in Story, *Miscellaneous Writings*, pp. 66, 340–378, 615–617. For an account of Story's fears of industrialization and the rise of great, unruly cities, most notably with reference to the Dartmouth College case, see Dunne, *Justice Joseph Story*, pp. 204–205; also Story, *Commentaries on the Law of Bailments with Illustrations from the Civil and the Foreign Law*, 3rd ed. (Boston: Charles C. Little and James Brown, 1843), p. 16.

3. Elizabeth Kelly Bauer, *Commentaries on the Constitution, 1790–1860* (New York: Columbia University Press, 1952), pp. 143–144; on instruction, see Story to Francis Lieber, April 10, 1836, and Story to John Berrien, Feb. 14, 1843, in *Life and Letters*, vol. 2, pp. 230, 433. Calhoun repeatedly insisted that a congressman who could not in good conscience yield to the wishes of his constituents ought to resign. In response to accusations by northern opponents, he also repeatedly declared himself a friend of suffrage extension—see, for example, vol. 17.

4. See especially "The Science of Government," in Story, *Miscellaneous Writings*, pp. 622, 629.

5. "Literary Tendencies of the Times," in Story, *Miscellaneous Writings*, p. 743.

6. Newmyer, *Joseph Story*, p. 164.

7. On Calhoun's theological liberalism, see Wiltse, *Calhoun*, vol. 3, pp. 288–289.

8. For the reactions of Story and Kent, see Dunne, *Justice Joseph Story*, pp. 331–333; for an illustration of the depth of Story's outrage, see Story to Richard Peters, July 6, 1844, in *Life and Letters of Joseph Story*, vol. 2, pp. 482–483.

9. The principal exception among southern theorists was the idiosyncratic Thomas Cooper, who was born in England and did not move to South Carolina until late in life. For Story's views, see Story to Edward Everett, Sept. 15, 1824, and "Christianity as a Part of the Common Law" (written in 1811 but not published until 1833), in *Life and Letters of Joseph Story*, vol. 1, pp. 429–430 (letter) and pp. 431–435 (text); see also W. W. Story's discussion of the Girard case and Kent's agreement with Story's views, vol. 2, pp. 461–470. See also "Value and Importance of Legal Studies" (1829), in Story, *Miscellaneous Writings*, p. 517.

10. Calhoun to A. D. Wallace, Dec. 17, 1840, in *Papers of John C. Calhoun*, vol. 15, p. 389. The so-called *Exposition and Protest* was in fact two separate documents, the first largely written by Calhoun. See Clyde Wilson's editorial comments in vol. 10.

11. As quoted in R. K. Matthews, *Radical Politics of Thomas Jefferson: A Revisionist View* (Lawrence: University of Kansas Press, 1986), p. 19. Matthews has made a strong case for Jefferson's radicalism, of which he strongly approves, although a case could be made for Jefferson's own southern brand of conservatism, especially on constitutional issues. Dumas Malone, Jefferson's great modern biographer, interprets Jefferson's view of history as classically liberal. See *Jefferson and His Times*, 6 vols. (Boston: Little, Brown, 1962–1981), vol. 6, pp. 137–138, 200–212. Jefferson never did reconcile the antagonistic principles or at least political preferences in his own thought. Forrest McDonald, in what surely ranks as the most curious compliment ever to appear as a bookjacket blurb, praised Matthews for having demonstrated, if inadvertently, that Jefferson was "precisely the wild-eyed political quack that the 'high Federalists' understood him to be." For what it may be worth, the Communist Party sponsored the "Jefferson School of Social Science" in New York, and Ezra Pound began a hymn to Jefferson's political thought by praising his insistence that the earth belongs to the living. See Pound's unabashedly profascist *Jefferson and/or Mussolini: L'Idea Statale—Fascism as I See It* (New York: Liveright Publishing, 1935), p. 115.

12. John Taylor, *An Inquiry into the Principles and Policy of the Government of the United States*, ed. Loren Baritz (Indianapolis: Bobbs-Merrill, 1969), pp. 60, 63, 66, 70, 85–88, 129 (on Paine), 220, 541–542. Jefferson largely agreed with Taylor's historical readings. See Malone, *Jefferson and His Times*, vol. 6, pp. 213–214.

13. Taylor's admiration for Godwin, although cushioned by a slashing criticism of his social leveling, should therefore come as no surprise: Taylor, *Inquiry*, Section 7, pp. 440–471. (If I seem to be saying that, for all of Taylor's undeniable talent and flashes of intellectual power, he was at bottom a muddlehead, I throw myself upon the mercy of the court of public opinion.)

14. Taylor, *Inquiry*, pp. 58–59, 108, 223, 230–231, 275–276.

15. Ibid., pp. 16–17, 32–36, 112, 121. See Marx, *Capital*, 3 vols. (Moscow: Foreign Languages Publishing House, 1961–1962), vol. 1, pp. 71–83.

16. Nathan Dane, Story's patron and mentor, fell into the same error, blaming Jefferson for having led Virginians and Carolinians into a Platonism incompatible with sound legal thinking. See Bauer, *Commentaries on the Constitution*, p. 279, n. 104. Dane's attribution of Platonism to Jefferson cannot be credited, and he apparently did not notice that Aristotle, not Plato, grounded subsequent southern political thought.

17. Elizabeth Fox-Genovese and Eugene D. Genovese, "Political Virtue and

the Lessons of the French Revolution: The View from the Slaveholding South," in *Virtue, Commerce, and Corruption,* ed. Richard Matthews (Bethlehem, Pa.: Lehigh University Press, forthcoming).

18. Calhoun to Mrs. Thomas G. Clemson, April 28, 1848, in Calhoun, *Correspondence Addressed to John C. Calhoun, 1837–1849,* ed. Chauncey S. Boucher and Robert P. Brooks, in *Annual Report of the American Historical Association (1899),* (Washington, D.C.: American Historical Association, 1900), vol. 2, p. 752.

19. "Speech on the Revenue Bill," Jan. 31, 1816, in *Papers of John C. Calhoun,* vol. 1, p. 329.

20. *Papers of John C. Calhoun,* vol. 1, p. 325; for Randolph's response see editor's note, vol. 1, p. 331, n. 123.

21. "Second Speech on the Bill for Admission of Michigan," Jan. 5, 1837, in *Papers of John C. Calhoun,* vol. 13, p. 349.

22. Taylor, *Inquiry,* p. 79. Taylor foreshadowed both the southern-conservative and radical left-wing (Critical Legal Studies) criticisms of equality before the law as being no protection of the poor and weak against the rich and strong: *Inquiry,* p. 92.

23. M. E. Bradford, "On Remembering Who We Are: A Political Credo," in M. E. Bradford, *Remembering Who We Are: Observations of a Southern Conservative* (Athens: University of Georgia Press, 1985), pp. 11–12.

24. Johann Huizinga, *The Waning of the Middle Ages: A Study of the Forms of Life, Thought and Art in France and the Netherlands in the Fourteenth and Fifteenth Centuries* (London: Edward Arnold, 1963), pp. 53–54. Much of what Robert A. Nisbet says of the feudal roots of European conservatism applies to southern conservatism as well. Nisbet largely ignores southern conservatism except for reference to Weaver, but his little book is invaluable for an understanding of this subject—and much else. See *Conservatism: Dream and Reality* (Minneapolis: University of Minnesota Press, 1968).

25. William Freehling, *Road to Disunion,* vol. 1, *Secessionists at Bay, 1776–1854* (New York: Oxford University Press, 1990), p. 43.

26. Henry St. George Tucker, *Lectures on Government* (Charlottesville: J. Alexander, 1844), pp. 31, 34.

27. Ibid., pp. 51–52. See also David M. Cobin, *Henry St. George Tucker: Jurist, Teacher, Citizen, 1740–1848* (Stephens City, Va.: Commercial Press, 1992).

28. Here I have especially benefited from the criticism of Clyde Wilson, notwithstanding our disagreements over the specifics and ramifications.

29. G. W. Featherstonhaugh, *Canoe Voyage Up the Minnay Sotor*, 2 vols. (St. Paul, Minn.: Minnesota Historical Society, 1970; orig. pub. 1847), p. 249; James Stirling, *Letters from the Slave States*, (New York: Negro Universities Press, 1969; orig. pub. 1857), pp. 75–76, 129.

30. Taylor, *Inquiry*, pp. 74–75.

31. John C. Calhoun, *A Disquisition on Government and Selections from the Discourse* (Indianapolis: Bobbs-Merrill, 1953), p. 45. Calhoun worked out his constitutional theories, as well as his ideas on society, politics, and economics, in speeches on practical questions—for example, the Fort Hill Address of 1831, the reply to Webster on the Force Bill (1833), and his reply to Andrew Jackson's protest (1834). Some of the most important of these and other documents, which are essential to an understanding of his short discourses, may be found in Clyde Wilson's edition of *The Essential Calhoun*.

32. "Discourse on the Constitution," in John C. Calhoun, *Union and Liberty: The Political Philosophy of John C. Calhoun*, ed. Ross M. Lence (Indianapolis: Liberty Fund, 1992), pp. 81–82, 105, 120–121, 132, 140–141. John Randolph spoke in somewhat different terms, but it is not clear that he meant anything substantially different despite his famous witticism that to ask a state to surrender part of her sovereignty is to ask a lady to surrender part of her chastity.

33. Essay addressed to William Smith, July 1843, in *The Essential Calhoun*, p. 50; see also *Works of John C. Calhoun*, vol. 6, pp. 221—227. Still, political leaders, as well as some theorists, easily slipped into assertions of natural-rights doctrine when their cause required. Jefferson Davis, without much philosophical reflection, saw it as a bulwark against despotism, referring to the federal government's invasion of the natural and inalienable rights of man, subjugation of the sovereignty of the people, and monstrous usurpation of powers, not granted in the Constitution. See Jefferson Davis, *The Rise and Fall of the Confederate Government*, 2 vols. (New York: Thomas Yoseloff, 1958), vol. 2, p. 762. Dixon H. Lewis of Alabama, a staunch Calhounite, argued that the Constitution must be upheld against natural-rights doctrine, but he added that that doctrine could be invoked to support revolutionary opposition to extreme oppression. See Lewis to Joseph A. Scoville, May 30, 1842, in *Papers of John C. Calhoun*, vol. 16, pp. 265–266.

34. Charles Royster, *The Destructive War: William Tecumseh Sherman, Stonewall Jackson, and the Americans* (New York: Knopf, 1991), pp. 282–283. Edmund Wilson, *Patriotic Gore: Studies in the Literature of the American Civil War* (New York: Oxford University Press, 1962), pp. 763, 766, 775.

35. Joseph Glover Baldwin, *Party Leaders: Sketches of Thomas Jefferson, Alex'r*

Hamilton, Andrew Jackson, Henry Clay, and John Randolph of Roanoke (New York: Appleton, 1868), p. 87.

36. Vernon L. Parrington, *Main Currents of American Thought*, 3 vols. (New York: Harcourt, Brace, 1927), vol. 2, p. 84; see also his perceptive remarks, vol. 2, pp. 12, 68–69, 88.

37. Ibid., *Main Currents*, vol. 2, p. 93. Albert J. Beveridge, staunchly defending the nationalist interpretation of the Constitution but disgusted by the Alien and Sedition Acts, commented, "Thus, unhappily, democracy marched arm in arm with State Rights, while Nationalism found itself the intimate companion of a narrow, bigoted, and retrograde conservatism." *The Life of John Marshall*, 4 vols. (Boston: Houghton Mifflin, 1916–1919), vol. 3, p. 48.

38. William Rawle, *A View of the Constitution of the United States of America* (Philadelphia: H. C. Carey and I. Lea, 1825); Henry Baldwin, *A General View of the Origin and Nature of the Constitution and Government of the United States* (Philadelphia: John C. Clark, 1837).

39. William B. Hesseltine, *Lincoln and the War Governors* (New York: Knopf, 1948).

40. See especially Davis, *Rise and Fall*, vol. 1, pp. 167, 409–410. Parrington did not err in describing Alexander Stephens' postwar constitutional treatise as "one of the most notable studies in the origin of the Constitution that we have." See *Main Currents*, vol. 2, p. 84; Alexander Stephens, *A Constitutional View of the Late War between the States; Its Causes, Character, Conduct and Results. Presented in a Series of Colloquia at Liberty Hall*, 2 vols. (New York: Kraus Reprint Co., 1970).

41. Lorman Ratner, *Powder Keg: Northern Opposition to the Antislavery Movement, 1831–1840* (New York: Basic Books, 1968), p. 54; "Remarks of Stephen F. Miller, Esq., on the Southern Question," in Miller, *The Bench and Bar of Georgia: Memoirs and Sketches*, 2 vols. (Philadelphia: Lippincott, 1858), vol. 2, pp. 399, 404.

42. Calhoun to Duff Green, Sept. 20, 1834, in *Papers of John C. Calhoun*, vol. 12, p. 363.

43. See, e.g., Merrill D. Peterson, *The Jefferson Image in the American Mind* (New York: Oxford University Press, 1962), pp. 212–213.

44. Abel P. Upshur, *A Brief Enquiry into the True Nature and Character of Our Federal Government: Being a Review of Judge Story's Commentaries on the Constitution of the United States* (Philadelphia: John Campbell, 1863; orig. pub. 1840); Henry St. George Tucker, *Lectures on Constitutional Law for the Use of the Law Class at the University of Virginia* (Richmond: Sheperd and Colin, 1843). Waddy

Thompson, a Unionist, justified state rights for the United States as necessary to a sprawling, sectionally torn republic but he cautioned Mexico against them. Mexico, he noted, is homogeneous and could profit by considerable centralization of power. Waddy Thompson, *Recollections of Mexico* (New York: Wiley and Putnam, 1846), pp. 58–59.

45. For Trescot, see Eugene D. Genovese, *The Slaveholders' Dilemma: Freedom and Progress in Southern Conservative Thought, 1820–1860* (Columbia: University of South Carolina Press, 1991), ch. 3, and references cited therein, especially to the contributions of David Moltke-Hansen.

46. "Discourse on the Constitution," in Calhoun, *Union and Liberty*, pp. 252–254; "Remarks at Dinner at Shocco Springs, N.C.," in *Papers of John C. Calhoun*, vol. 16, pp. 440–441.

47. Arthur M. Schlesinger, Jr., *Age of Jackson* (Boston: Little, Brown, 1946), p. 19.

48. Calhoun to Frederick W. Symmes, July 26, 1831, for publication in the *Messenger* and generally known as "The Fort Hill Address," in *Papers of John C. Calhoun*, vol. 11, pp. 413–440; "Discourse on the Constitution," in *Union and Liberty*, pp. 278–279, 284–285. Calhoun may well have also had Sparta in mind as a model for his doctrine of concurrent majority, but Sparta's reputation as an oppressive state militated against its being cited favorably in the Old South and in America generally. On the Spartan version of dual power, see Paul Rahe, *Republics, Ancient and Modern: Classical Republicanism and the American Revolution* (Chapel Hill: University of North Carolina Press, 1992), pp. 166, 184.

49. Or as Ralph Gabriel has put it, Calhoun was trying to save the very principle of a single American nationality. See *The Course of American Democratic Thought*, 3rd ed. (New York: Greenwood Press, 1986), p. 109.

50. P. B. Knupfer makes this point well in *The Union as It Is: Constitutional Unionism and Sectional Compromise, 1787–1861* (Chapel Hill: University of North Carolina Press, 1991), p. 107. In fact, George Mason had preceded Madison in this view.

51. Cathy D. Matson and Peter S. Onuf, *A Union of Interests: Political and Economic Thought in Revolutionary America* (Lawrence: University of Kansas Press, 1990), pp. 110–111.

52. Calhoun to Andrew Pickens Calhoun, Feb. 23, 1848, in *Correspondence of John C. Calhoun*, p. 744; "Discourse on Government," in Calhoun, *Union and Liberty*, especially pp. 274–275. John Randolph took a different view of the significance of the Northwest Ordinance. As chairman of a congressional committee that was considering Indiana's request in 1803 to be allowed to retain

slavery, he ruled the request "highly dangerous and inexpedient." See Mary S. Locke, *Anti-Slavery in America from the Introduction of African Slaves to the Prohibition of the Slave Trade, 1619–1808* (Gloucester, Mass.: Peter Smith, rpt. 1965), pp. 158–159.

53. "Discourse on the Constitution," in Calhoun, *Union and Liberty*, p. 88.

54. Stephens, *Constitutional View*, vol. 1, p. 530.

55. "Discourse on the Constitution," in Calhoun, *Union and Liberty*, pp. 88, 97, 99, 115, 212, 215. Stephens followed Calhoun on the distinction between allegiance and obedience. See *Constitutional View*, vol. 1, p. 25.

56. "Discourse on the Constitution," in Calhoun, *Union and Liberty*, pp. 92–99.

57. Stephens, in *Constitutional View*, and Jefferson Davis, in *The Rise and Fall of the Confederate Government*, 2 vols. (New York: Thomas Yoseloff, 1958), both argue this point forcefully and repeatedly, the former more effectively than the latter.

58. David Potter, normally one of our surest guides to southern history, curiously asserts that antebellum southerners rejected the theory of concurrent majority while employing it as a tactic. See David M. Potter, *The South and the Concurrent Majority*, ed. Don E. Fehrenbacher and Carl N. Degler (Baton Rouge: Louisiana State University Press, 1972). In fact, a good many leading southern political leaders, including Jefferson Davis, embraced the theory but doubted that they could bring the North to accept it.

59. Charles H. Ambler, *Sectionalism in Virginia* (Chicago: University of Chicago Press, 1910), p. 152.

60. "Speech on Internal Improvements," Feb. 4, 1817, in *Papers of John C. Calhoun*, vol. 1, p. 403.

61. "The South and the American Union," in Richard M. Weaver, *The Southern Essays of Richard Weaver*, ed. George M. Curtis III and James J. Thompson, Jr. (Indianapolis: Liberty Press, 1987), p. 233.

62. Taylor, *Inquiry*, pp. 83–84.

63. Orestes Brownson to John C. Calhoun, Oct. 13, 1841, in *Papers of John C. Calhoun*, vol. 15, p. 791.

64. Calhoun to Robert S. Garnett, July 3, 1824, in *Papers of John C. Calhoun*, vol. 9, p. 198; "Discourse on the Constitution," in *Union and Liberty*, pp. 161–164.

65. See the astute evaluations in Bauer, *Commentaries on the Constitution*, especially pp. 21, 29, 211. For a strong attempt to steer a middle course that wound up in support of the state-rights interpretation on the essentials, see

Henry Baldwin, *General View of the Constitution*. So pervasive was the opposition to a national consolidation designed to annihilate the power of states that even so staunch a nationalist as James Kent went to great lengths to deny any such intent, thereby making his own feeble claim to the search for a middle course. See Kent, *Commentaries on American Law*, 4 vols., 2nd ed. (New York: O. Halstead, 1832), vol. 1, p. 279.

66. Among Bradford's outstanding contributions to scholarship was his exploration of the thought and politics of the conservative Anti-Federalists, who opposed the Constitution for reasons in some important ways different from those of the more widely studied radicals. Bradford also established the link between the conservative Anti-Federalists and the Agrarians and their successors. See Bradford, *A Better Guide than Reason: Studies in the American Revolution* (La Salle, Ill.: Sherwood Sugden, 1979), pp. 59–76; idem, *A Worthy Company: Brief Lives of the Framers of the United States Constitution* (Marlborough, N.H.: Plymouth Rock Foundation, 1982); idem, *Remembering Who We Are*, pp. 13, 65; idem, *The Reactionary Imperative: Essays, Literary and Political* (Peru, Ill.: Sherwood Sugden, 1979), pp. 120–132; and Bradford's posthumously published *Original Intentions: On the Making and Ratification of the United States Constitution* (Athens: University of Georgia Press, 1993).

67. Richard Hofstadter has a brief but penetrating discussion of the southerners' miscalculation in *The American Political Tradition and the Men Who Made It* (New York: Knopf, 1948), pp. 86–91.

68. Lewis P. Simpson, *Mind and the American Civil War: A Meditation on Lost Causes* (Baton Rouge: Louisiana State University Press, 1989). Among the Agrarians, John Gould Fletcher suggested such an interpretation in his interesting comparison of American and Russian history, *The Two Frontiers: A Study in Historical Psychology* (New York: Coward-McCann, 1930), p. 302.

69. For an elaboration see Elizabeth Fox-Genovese, *Within the Plantation Household: Black and White Women of the Old South* (Chapel Hill: University of North Carolina Press, 1988), especially ch. 1; and Eugene D. Genovese, "'Our Family, White and Black': Family and Household in the Southern Slaveholders' World View," in Carol Bleser, *In Joy and in Sorrow: Women, Family, and Marriage in the Victorian South* (New York: Oxford University Press, 1991), pp. 69–87.

70. For Story on the immorality but legality of slavery, see, e.g., his *Commentaries on the Conflict of Laws, Foreign and Domestic, in Regard to Contracts, Rights, and Remedies, and Especially in Regard to Marriages, Divorces, Wills, Successions, and Judgments* (New York: Arno Press, 1972; orig. pub. 1834), pp. 26,

97, 103–104, 259. For his explanation of his course in *Prigg v. Pennsylvania*, see *Life and Letters*, vol. 2, pp. 381–398; and for an assessment, see Newmyer, *Joseph Story*, pp. 74–75, which quotes Story's letter to Nathaniel Williams, Feb. 22, 1815, on the extension of national power.

71. "Speech on Surveys for Roads and Canals," Jan. 30, 1824, text in Russell Kirk, *John Randolph of Roanoke: A Study in American Politics*, 3rd ed. (Indianapolis: Liberty Fund, 1978), pp. 413–439 (words quoted from p. 433). Nathaniel Macon of North Carolina, among others, used this argument when attacking internal improvements and other federal measures. See, e.g., Robert M. Calhoon, *Evangelicals and Conservatives in the Early South* (Columbia: University of South Carolina Press, 1988), p. 168.

72. Thus, Tate, in his biography of Jefferson Davis and elsewhere, assailed the Old South's egalitarian and democratic streak as wrong on principle and self-defeating. See Mark Malvasi, "Risen from the Bloody Sod: Recovering the Southern Tradition" (diss., University of Rochester, 1991), especially p. 183.

73. Herbert Agar and Allen Tate, eds., *Who Owns America? A New Declaration of Independence* (Boston: Houghton Mifflin, 1936).

74. John Randolph, quoted in Kirk, *John Randolph of Roanoke*, p. 46.

75. Bradford, *Better Guide than Reason*, pp. 29, 30; idem, *Remembering Who We Are*, p. 11; Richard M. Weaver, *The Southern Tradition at Bay* (Washington, D.C.: Regnery Gateway, 1989), pp. 18–21. This charge that the doctrine of equality of opportunity must end with an attempt to legislate equality of result is borne out by the Supreme Court's decisions on affirmative action, although there has been a lot of backing-and-filling along the way. See Herman Belz, "Affirmative Action," in Kermit Hall, ed., *The Oxford Companion to the Supreme Court* (New York: Oxford University Press, 1992), pp. 18–22.

76. Weaver, *Southern Tradition at Bay*, p. 160.

77. Most of the Agrarians believed in the inferiority of blacks. Allen Tate's defense of a white racial dictatorship is nonetheless illuminating. See Malvasi, "Risen from the Bloody Sod," p. 112.

78. Allen Tate to Donald Davidson, Aug. 10, 1929, quoted in Lewis P. Simpson, "The Southern Republic of Letters and *I'll Take My Stand*," in William C. Havard and Walter Sullivan, eds., *A Band of Prophets: The Vanderbilt Agrarians after Fifty Years* (Baton Rouge: Louisiana State University Press), pp. 68–69.

79. Frank L. Owsley, "The Foundations of Democracy," in Agar and Tate, eds., *Who Owns America?* p. 61; Owsley, *State Rights in the Confederacy* (Chicago: University of Chicago Press, 1925). See also Andrew Lytle, *From Eden to*

Babylon: The Social and Political Essays of Andrew Nelson Lytle, ed. M. E. Bradford (Washington, D.C.: Regnery Gateway, 1990), pp. 75, 126–127, 133; Donald Davidson, *Regionalism and Nationalism in the United States: The Attack on Leviathan* (New Brunswick, N.J.: Transaction Publishers, 1991).

80. Thomas Roderick Dew, *A Digest of the Laws, Customs, Manners, Institutions of the Ancient and Modern Nations* (New York: Appleton, 1884), p. 202.

81. Dew, *Digest*, pp. 203, 204.

82. Bradford, "Preface," in *Remembering Who We Are*, p. xi.

83. Bradford, "On Remembering Who We Are: A Southern Credo," in *Remembering Who We Are*, pp. 3–17; idem, *Reactionary Imperative*, pp. 101–114.

84. Bradford, "On Remembering Who We Are: A Southern Credo," in *Remembering Who We Are*, p. 12.

85. Schumpeter declared for Catholic social policy in "The Future of Private Enterprise in the Face of Modern Socialistic Tendencies." See Joseph Schumpeter, *The Economics and Sociology of Capitalism*, ed. Richard Swedberg (Princeton: Princeton University Press, 1991), pp. 401–405.

86. Joseph A. Schumpeter, *Capitalism, Socialism, and Democracy*, 3rd ed. (New York: Harper and Row, 1950).

3. Property and Power

1. Allen Tate, "The Profession of Letters in the South," *Reactionary Essays on Poetry and Ideas* (New York: Charles Scribner's Sons, 1936), pp. 155, 147. The focus on the yeomanry seriously undermined the effort by Tate and others to forge a modern southern conservatism. See Elizabeth Fox-Genovese, *Southern Conservatism and the Critique of Modernity* (Tuscaloosa: University of Alabama Press, 1991). Lewis P. Simpson, whose roots are in the southern tradition, has criticized with deep insight and learning the evasion of the centrality of slavery in the work of the Agrarians and their successors. See especially Lewis P. Simpson, *The Dispossessed Garden: Pastoral and History in Southern Literature* (Athens: University of Georgia Press, 1975); and idem, *The Brazen Face of History: Studies in the Literary Consciousness in America* (Baton Rouge: Louisiana State University Press, 1980). Among the Agrarians, John Gould Fletcher did recognize the centrality of slavery to the South's social, political, and constitutional order. See Fletcher, *The Two Frontiers: A Study in Historical Psychology* (New York: Coward-McCann, 1930), p. 299.

2. Richard Weaver, *Ideas Have Consequences* (Chicago: University of Chicago Press, 1948), p. 132.

3. Southern conservatives have ignored the critical work of Alfred Chandler, among others. See especially Chandler, *The Visible Hand: Managerial Revolution in American Business* (Cambridge, Mass.: Harvard University Press, 1977).

4. See the essays of Lyle Lanier, Frank Lawrence Owsley, and Donald Davidson in Herbert Agar and Allen Tate, eds., *Who Owns America? A New Declaration of Independence* (Boston: Houghton Mifflin, 1936). Their proposal has recently been revived by Clyde Wilson, among other southern conservatives. See Wilson, "Restoring the Republic," *Chronicles: A Magazine of American Culture* (June 1993).

5. A dangerous nationalism, not to say chauvinism, provided the framework for the right-wing coalition, but that is a matter for a separate and careful analysis.

6. "The Week," *National Review* (March 16, 1992), p. 10.

7. The ideological split may, however, be narrowing, for many of the libertarians in question seem to be moving onto more traditionally conservative ground. Whether they can sustain themselves there while holding to their free-market economics remains doubtful.

8. Unsigned review in *G. K. Chesterton's Weekly*. I am indebted to William Blissett for this item, which appears in "G. K. Chesterton: Pickwickian Liberal," a paper he delivered at a conference on the Agrarians and the Distributists, held at Louisiana State University in 1992. I also wish to thank Dermot Quinn and Cleanth Brooks for letting me see the fine papers they delivered at that conference. Hillaire Belloc probably has had a greater impact than Chesterton on southern conservatives, who especially admire his book *The Servile State* (New York: Henry Holt, 1946).

9. Louis B. Wright, "Myth-Makers and the South's Dilemma," in Allen Tate, ed., *A Southern Vanguard: The John Peale Bishop Memorial Volume* (New York: Prentice-Hall, 1947), pp. 145–147; George Rogers, Jr., "A Southern Political Tradition," in Fifteen Southerners, *Why the South Will Survive* (Athens: University of Georgia Press, 1981), p. 89.

10. M. E. Bradford, "What We Can Know for Certain: Frank Owsley and the Recovery of Southern History," in *The Reactionary Imperative: Essays Literary and Political* (Peru, Ill.: Sherwood Sugden, 1990), pp. 179–180.

11. Tate to Lincoln Kirstein, quoted in Mark Malvasi, "Risen from the Bloody Sod: Recovering the Southern Tradition" (diss., University of Rochester, 1991), p. 112. Malvasi has an excellent discussion of the racial attitudes of the Agrarians. Kirstein was then editing *Hound and Horn*. He subsequently went on to a distinguished career as a ballet impresario in New York.

12. The identification of racism with fascism is a dangerously misleading

half-truth, for racism has done nicely in democratic regimes. Mussolini's fascism had a racist tendency but should not be confused with Hitler's overtly racist ideology and practice. Mussolini, like Giovanni Gentile, the principal fascist philosopher, considered racism stupid. To be sure, Mussolini, who was himself never entirely free of racist attitudes, cynically took the racist road politically when he entered into his alliance with Hitler. However distasteful the white-supremicist regime in South Africa, it never qualified as fascist. But then, in recent years we have been treated to the silliness that describes military dictatorships like Pinochet's in Chile and Jaruzelski's in Poland as fascist. One would think that even superficial writers would know that fascism and military dictatorship are mutually exclusive.

The Agrarians, along with T. S. Eliot, came under especially heavy fire during the 1950s for alleged fascism in their promotion of the "New Criticism." For a brief discussion see George Core, "Agrarianism, Criticism, and the Academy," in William C. Havard and Walter Sullivan, eds., *A Band of Prophets: The Vanderbilt Agrarians after Fifty Years* (Baton Rouge: Louisiana State University Press, 1982), pp. 134–145. As a Communist college student, I was puzzled by the Party's attacks on Eliot for being—by some miracle—simultaneously a fascist and an ivory-tower poet. I am pleased to report, however, that I had the pleasure of taking Murray Young's course on modern poetry, in which Eliot was treated with the respect he deserved. Professor Young, a Communist himself, was purged from the faculty at Brooklyn College shortly thereafter. Sidney Hook was not alone in erroneously assuming that Communist professors followed the party line in their classrooms. Many did not.

13. For a responsible and distressingly accurate analysis of the points of convergence, see especially A. James Gregor, *The Ideology of Fascism: The Rationale of Totalitarianism* (New York: Free Press, 1969); and idem, *Contemporary Radical Ideologies* (New York: Random House, 1969).

14. Richard M. Weaver, *The Southern Essays of Richard Weaver*, ed. George M. Curtis III and James J. Thompson, Jr. (Indianapolis: Liberty Press, 1987), p. 169; also pp. 183–187. For Weaver's critique of fascism, see also *Ideas Have Consequences*, pp. 55–56, 110, 114, 120; and idem *Visions of Order: The Cultural Crisis of Our Time* (Baton Rouge: Louisiana State University Press, 1964), pp. 13–15.

15. "Breve preludio," *Opera omnia di Benito Mussolini*, ed. Edoardo and Duilio Susmel, 43 vols. (Florence: La Fenice, 1956), vol. 17, p. 221.

16. "Fascismo: Dottrina," *Enciclopedia italiana dei scienza ed arti*, 36 vols. (Treves: Edizioni Istituto Trescanni, 1929–1939), vol. 14, pp. 847–851. This article was signed by Mussolini, although the first part was written by Gentile.

Gentile and Mussolini were implicitly assailing the alternate concept of *lo stato etico* advanced by Benedetto Croce, Italy's great liberal philosopher.

17. Contrast the views of Gentile, who served as Mussolini's first minister of education, with those of southern conservatives from James Henley Thornwell to John Gould Fletcher, Richard Weaver, and Thomas Fleming. Gentile wrote extensively on education. A brief statement of his views, translated into English, can be found in his book *The Genesis and Structure of Society*, trans. H. S. Harris (Urbana: University of Illinois Press, 1960), pp. 177–179. John Gould Fletcher, "Education, Past and Present," in Twelve Southerners, *I'll Take My Stand: The South and the Agrarian Tradition* (New York: Harper, 1930), pp. 92–121; Weaver, *Ideas Have Consequences*, pp. 8, 14, 41, 49–52, 92–97, 105, 165–168; Weaver, *Visions of Order*, pp. 114–117, 150–151; Thomas Fleming, "Southern Schooling and the Ancient Wisdom," in Fifteen Southerners, *Why the South Will Survive*, pp. 105–118.

18. *Opera omnia di Benito Mussolini*, vol. 21, p. 425. See also Gregor, *Ideology of Fascism*, pp. 154, 234. John Lukacs has reminded me in private correspondence of a point he has made effectively in his books. Mussolini's philosophical doctrine of the state as the supreme ideal to which the individual must subordinate himself flows from Renaissance traditions. In its political as well as philosophical ramifications, it is far removed from Hitler's National Socialist doctrine of the centrality of the *Volk* and the artificiality of the state.

19. The doctrine of the personal as political constitutes an essential running thread in Gentile's political theory. See the pointed remarks in Gentile, *Origin and Structure of Society*, 176–178. See also "Fascismo: Dottrina."

20. Weaver, "The South and the Revolution of Nihilism," *Southern Essays*, pp. 183, 187.

21. Richard M. Weaver, *The Southern Tradition at Bay* (Washington, D.C.: Regnery Gateway, 1989), p. 73. Finally, we have a much needed first-rate study of Henry Hughes. See Douglas Ambrose, "'The Man for Times Coming': The Life and Thought of Henry Hughes" (diss.: State University of New York at Binghamton, 1991), a revised version of which will soon be published.

Parenthetically, southern conservatives have had a hard time sorting out their attitudes toward the Populists, fearing their social radicalism and the threat posed by the very existence of their movement to the unity of the community, but admiring their opposition to big business and their defense of the small farmer. And when the Watsons and Tillmans emerged as race-baiting demagogues, the more genteel of the conservatives drew back in disgust. The result in the complex politics of the South has been the failure of southern conservatism to confront the Populist experience and to formulate a critique of its strengths and weaknesses. Bradford, however, did take up this subject in "Word from the Forks of the Creek: The Revolution and the Populist Heritage," *A Better Guide than Reason: Studies in the American Revolution* (La Salle, Ill.: Sherwood Sugden, 1979), pp. 59–76. Also Havard and Sullivan, "Introduction," in *Band of Prophets*, p. 5.

22. Albert Einstein invited Sigmund Freud to offer an analysis of the prospects for world peace. Freud, as might have been expected, was not optimistic. In a response that occasioned some surprise, Einstein, although cautiously optimistic, agreed with Freud's claim that there is an aggressive instinct in human beings. See Albert Einstein and Sigmund Freud, *Why War?* trans. Stuart Gilbert (Geneva: International Institute of Intellectual Co-Operation, League of Nations, 1933).

23. Weaver, "The Tennessee Agrarians," in *Southern Essays*, p. 12; also, idem, "Southern Chivalry and Total War," p. 169. See also Bradford, *Reactionary Imperative*, pp. 94–95, 205–217. The language used by Pope John Paul II in his critique of scientism and its outcome in the threat of nuclear war strongly resembles that of the Agrarians, Weaver, and Bradford. See the encyclical *Centesimus Annus* (Washington: U.S. Catholic Conference, 1981), no. 18.

Weaver's stance here recalls that of his German contemporary Carl Schmitt, who sought to reassert Vattel's effort to accept war with limits to its legitimate goals and practices—that is, to treat war as a limited quarrel between states rather than as an ideological crusade. Alas, Schmitt eventually joined the Nazi Party, apparently in the forlorn hope that he could help civilize the powers-that-be. Notwithstanding Schmitt's services to the Nazis, his political theory proved largely unassimilable to their ideology. See Paul A. Gottfried, *Carl Schmitt: Politics and Theory* (New York: Greenwood Press, 1990), pp. 9–10, 27, 80–81.

24. Gentile, *Genesis and Structure of Society*, p. 164. Gentile, here and elsewhere, seems to have made concessions to those fascist intransigents who berated him as a closet liberal, but on this issue the intransigents, not Gentile, set the party line.

25. See *Chronicles: A Magazine of American Culture*, the issues during the war in the Persian Gulf.

26. Reed, "The Same Old Stand," in Fifteen Southerners, *Why the South Will Survive*, pp. 21–22.

27. For a critical discussion of Owsley's views, see Reed, "For Dixieland: The

Sectionalism of *I'll Take My Stand,*" in Havard and Sullivan, eds., *Band of Prophets,* p. 50.

28. A caveat: A left-wing friend who read a draft of this book remarked, "I'd like to agree with your discussion of universities, but alas, I don't. I think the real universities of the future will probably be found in basements, backrooms, and garages—and will probably be illegal." He may well be right. But here, I am discussing principles and possibilities, not prophesying. The current situation is appalling and will probably get worse. But as my friend would agree, that probability is no excuse for fatalism and apathy.

29. For an elaboration, see Eugene D. Genovese, "Critical Legal Studies as Radical Politics and World View," *Yale Journal of Law and Humanities* 3 (Winter 1991): 131–156, from which I have lifted some passages.

30. Francis Fukuyama, *The End of History and the Last Man* (New York: Free Press, 1992), p. 328.

31. Yes, trust in their own free will. The widespread notion that the South was conquered by Calvinist predestinarianism is a figment of historian's imagination, as Elizabeth Fox-Genovese and I shall try to demonstrate in a forthcoming book on the life and mind of the slaveholders.

32. Quoted in Richard Weaver, "Lee the Philosopher," *Southern Essays,* pp. 179–180.

Acknowledgments

I was honored to be invited by the Charles Warren Center of Harvard University to deliver the William E. Massey Sr. Lectures in the History of American Civilization and am grateful to Alan Heimert, Christine McFadden, and Tom Augst, as well as to the faculty and students of Harvard and to the Cambridge community, for their hospitality and stimulating intellectual challenges. I am indebted to Aida Donald of Harvard University Press for her encouragement and guidance in the preparation of the manuscript, and to Maria Ascher for her excellent editing.

I am indebted to friends from inside and outside the southern conservative tradition—from, as it were, the Right to the Left—for painstaking criticism of the manuscript: Stanley L. Engerman, Louis A. Ferleger, John Lukacs, Mark Malvasi, Ellen McDonald, Forrest McDonald, Robert L. Paquette, John Shelton Reed, Lewis P. Simpson, Clyde Wilson, and Harold D. Woodman. I owe a special debt to Mark Malvasi, from whose admirable doctoral dissertation, "Risen from the Bloody Sod: Recovering the Southern Tradition" (University of Rochester, 1991), I have drawn freely. Gore Vidal graciously agreed to read the manuscript of a lecture that served as the pilot for this book. With extraordinary generosity to a man he has never met, he offered an extensive commentary on a paper that,

I fear, was not to his taste. John Merriman checked the quotations and references, rescued me from careless errors, and shared with me his knowledge of the religious Right.

I was privileged to get considerable criticism of early versions of Chapter 1, which were presented as lectures at the University of South Carolina (Department of History), the University of Toronto (Department of Government), and Harvard University (Department of Government), and at my alma mater, Brooklyn College (the Wolfe Institute and the Department of Sociology), where I had the honor to deliver the annual Charles Lawrence Memorial Lecture.

The editors of the *Yale Journal of Law and the Humanities* have graciously consented to let me lift some portions of my article "Critical Legal Studies as Radical Politics and Ideology," which appeared in volume 3 (Winter 1991), pp. 131–156.

I wish to thank Jaroslav Pelikan for permission to quote from his translation of Goethe's *Faust* and his excellent remarks on tradition and traditionalism. This would appear to be as good a place as any to acknowledge my deep indebtedness to the corpus of his great scholarship.

Elizabeth Fox-Genovese, my collaborator for a quarter-century, has influenced my thought every step of the way. With her customary care she edited the manuscript for style and content and contributed more than I could repay. She has better reason than usual to insist that she is not responsible for the specifics of this book and especially for my refusal to cotton to "gender-neutral" language.

Index